CliffsNotes Finding What You Want on the Web

By Camille McCue

IN THIS BOOK

- Use Web directories and search engines to locate what you want on the Web
- Find information on the weather, news, and sports
- Skip going to the library — find out how to use reference materials online
- Enjoy yourself by finding out how to shop and play games on the Web
- Reinforce what you learn with CliffsNotes Review
- Find more about finding what you want on the Web in CliffsNotes Resource Center and online at www.cliffsnotes.com

IDG Books Worldwide, Inc.
An International Data Group Company
Foster City, CA • Chicago, IL • Indianapolis, IN • New York, NY

About the Author
Camille McCue sums up her career with three T's . . . technology, television, and teaching. She has worked 12 years in the high-tech arena for IBM, NASA, SAIC, and PBS (all the big acronyms!) using every imaginable telecommunications tool to help people learn about science and computing.

Publisher's Acknowledgments
Editorial
Senior Project Editor: Kelly Ewing
Acquisitions Editor: Steven H. Hayes
Technical Editor: Lee Musick
Production
Indexer: York Production Services, Inc.
Proofreader: York Production Services, Inc.
IDG Books Indianapolis Production Department

CliffsNotes™ Finding What You Want on the Web
Published by
IDG Books Worldwide, Inc.
An International Data Group Company
919 E. Hillsdale Blvd.
Suite 400
Foster City, CA 94404
www.idgbooks.com (IDG Books Worldwide Web site)
www.cliffsnotes.com (CliffsNotes Web site)

Note: If you purchased this book without a cover you should be aware that this book is stolen property. It was reported as "unsold and destroyed" to the publisher, and neither the author nor the publisher has received any payment for this "stripped book."

Copyright © 2000 IDG Books Worldwide, Inc. All rights reserved. No part of this book, including interior design, cover design, and icons, may be reproduced or transmitted in any form, by any means (electronic, photocopying, recording, or otherwise) without the prior written permission of the publisher.
Library of Congress Control Number: 00-101089
ISBN: 0-7645-8636-X
Printed in the United States of America
10 9 8 7 6 5 4 3 2 1
1O/RV/QX/QQ/IN
Distributed in the United States by IDG Books Worldwide, Inc.
Distributed by CDG Books Canada Inc. for Canada; by Transworld Publishers Limited in the United Kingdom; by IDG Norge Books for Norway; by IDG Sweden Books for Sweden; by IDG Books Australia Publishing Corporation Pty. Ltd. for Australia and New Zealand; by TransQuest Publishers Pte Ltd. for Singapore, Malaysia, Thailand, Indonesia, and Hong Kong; by Gotop Information Inc. for Taiwan; by ICG Muse, Inc. for Japan; by Intersoft for South Africa; by Eyrolles for France; by International Thomson Publishing for Germany, Austria and Switzerland; by Distribuidora Cuspide for Argentina; by LR International for Brazil; by Galileo Libros for Chile; by Ediciones ZETA S.C.R. Ltda. for Peru; by WS Computer Publishing Corporation, Inc., for the Philippines; by Contemporanea de Ediciones for Venezuela; by Express Computer Distributors for the Caribbean and West Indies; by Micronesia Media Distributor, Inc. for Micronesia; by Chips Computadoras S.A. de C.V. for Mexico; by Editorial Norma de Panama S.A. for Panama; by American Bookshops for Finland.
For general information on IDG Books Worldwide's books in the U.S., please call our Consumer Customer Service department at 800-762-2974. For reseller information, including discounts and premium sales, please call our Reseller Customer Service department at 800-434-3422.
For information on where to purchase IDG Books Worldwide's books outside the U.S., please contact our International Sales department at 317-596-5530 or fax 317-572-4002.
For consumer information on foreign language translations, please contact our Customer Service department at 1-800-434-3422, fax 317-572-4002, or e-mail rights@idgbooks.com.
For information on licensing foreign or domestic rights, please phone +1-650-653-7098.
For sales inquiries and special prices for bulk quantities, please contact our Order Services department at 800-434-3422 or write to the address above.
For information on using IDG Books Worldwide's books in the classroom or for ordering examination copies, please contact our Educational Sales department at 800-434-2086 or fax 317-572-4005.
For press review copies, author interviews, or other publicity information, please contact our Public Relations department at 650-653-7000 or fax 650-653-7500.
For authorization to photocopy items for corporate, personal, or educational use, please contact Copyright Clearance Center, 222 Rosewood Drive, Danvers, MA 01923, or fax 978-750-4470.

<u>**LIMIT OF LIABILITY/DISCLAIMER OF WARRANTY:**</u> THE PUBLISHER AND AUTHOR HAVE USED THEIR BEST EFFORTS IN PREPARING THIS BOOK. THE PUBLISHER AND AUTHOR MAKE NO REPRESENTATIONS OR WARRANTIES WITH RESPECT TO THE ACCURACY OR COMPLETENESS OF THE CONTENTS OF THIS BOOK AND SPECIFICALLY DISCLAIM ANY IMPLIED WARRANTIES OF MERCHANTABILITY OR FITNESS FOR A PARTICULAR PURPOSE. THERE ARE NO WARRANTIES WHICH EXTEND BEYOND THE DESCRIPTIONS CONTAINED IN THIS PARAGRAPH. NO WARRANTY MAY BE CREATED OR EXTENDED BY SALES REPRESENTATIVES OR WRITTEN SALES MATERIALS. THE ACCURACY AND COMPLETENESS OF THE INFORMATION PROVIDED HEREIN AND THE OPINIONS STATED HEREIN ARE NOT GUARANTEED OR WARRANTED TO PRODUCE ANY PARTICULAR RESULTS, AND THE ADVICE AND STRATEGIES CONTAINED HEREIN MAY NOT BE SUITABLE FOR EVERY INDIVIDUAL. NEITHER THE PUBLISHER NOR AUTHOR SHALL BE LIABLE FOR ANY LOSS OF PROFIT OR ANY OTHER COMMERCIAL DAMAGES, INCLUDING BUT NOT LIMITED TO SPECIAL, INCIDENTAL, CONSEQUENTIAL, OR OTHER DAMAGES.

Note: This book is intended to offer general information on finding what you want on the web. The author and publisher are not engaged in rendering legal, tax, accounting, investment, real estate, or similar professional services. Although legal, tax, accounting, investment, real estate, and similar issues addressed by this book have been checked with sources believed to be reliable, some material may be affected by changes in the laws and/or interpretation of laws since the manuscript in this book was completed. Therefore, the accuracy and completeness of the information provided herein and the opinions that have been generated are not guaranteed or warranted to produce particular results, and the strategies outlined in this book may not be suitable for every individual. If legal, tax, accounting, investment, real estate, or other expert advice is needed or appropriate, the reader is strongly encouraged to obtain the services of a professional expert.

Trademarks: Cliffs, CliffsNotes, and all related logos and trade dress are registered trademarks or trademarks of Cliffs Notes, Inc. in the United States and other countries. All other brand names and product names used in this book are trade names, service marks, trademarks, or registered trademarks of their respective holders. IDG Books Worldwide, Inc. and Cliffs Notes, Inc. are not associated with any product or vendor mentioned in this book.

 is a registered trademark under exclusive license to IDG Books Worldwide, Inc. from International Data Group, Inc.

Table of Contents

Introduction 1
   Why Do You Need This Book? 1
   How to Use This Book 2
   Don't Miss Our Web Site 3

Chapter 1: Getting Started 5
   Planning Your Search 5
      Knowing what's available online 6
      Is it free or is there a fee? 8
      Finding, not just surfing 9
      I found it! Now where exactly is it? 10
   Pick a Browser, Any Browser 10
      Navigating a browser window 11
      That little search button 13
      Bookmarking sites 13
   Gathering Your Search Tools 14
      Search engines 14
      Web directories 15

Chapter 2: Locating Information with Web Directories 16
   Deciding When to Use a Directory 16
   Knowing What's Listed — and What's Not 17
   Working through the Hierarchies 18
   Using the Directories 19
      Yahoo! 19
      Other free offerings 23
      Proprietary offerings 23

Chapter 3: Searching Strategically with Search Engines 24
   Deciding When to Use a Search Engine 24
   Guessing Intelligently at URLs 25
   Choosing a Search Engine 28
   Searching with a Keyword 30
      Reading search results 31
      Refining your search 33

Chapter 4: Finding Files and Downloading Documents 35
   Common File Types 35
   Locating Files 37
   Downloading and Using Files 38
   Getting Freeware 40
   Acquiring Cool Demos 41
   Purchasing Shareware 43

Chapter 5: Finding News, Weather, and Sports Information ...44
   Digging Up the Daily News 44
      Personalizing a page with your favorite news sources 45
      Reading your hometown newspaper online 46
      Getting alerts as headlines break 47
      Thumbing through online magazines 49
   Tracking the Weather 50
   Following Sports 52
      Personalizing a page with your favorite teams 52
      Watching and hearing streaming sportscasts 54

Chapter 6: Tracking Down and Interacting with People 55
   Locating Phone Numbers, Addresses, and More with White Pages 56
   Getting Information from Others via E-mail 57
      Setting up an e-mail account: a Hotmail example 58
      Signing into your Hotmail account 59
      Using and managing your Hotmail account 61
   Joining Common Interest Clubs 62
   Using Instant Messaging 63
      Downloading and installing an IM: an ICQ example 65
      Using ICQ 66
   Chatting in Chat Rooms 67

**Chapter 7: Looking It Up — Online Libraries and
Reference Materials** 69
   Digging into Online Dictionaries and Thesauri 71
   Retrieving Content from Encyclopedias, Maps, and Atlases 72
   Getting Cool Clips from Media Libraries 73
   Visiting the Library of Congress 74
   Finding Information on Everything with Virtual Reference Collection 75

Chapter 8: Getting Down to Business . . . and Government Information 77
Tracking Down Business and Financial Sites 78
Following News about Money 80
Investing Online 80
    Monitoring stocks with Yahoo! Messenger 81
    Going solo with Fidelity 82
Accessing Government Sites 82

Chapter 9: Shopping for Products and Services 86
Locating Goods for Sale 86
Purchasing Products Online 88
Buying and Selling via the Classifieds 91
Participating in Online Auctions 92
Making Travel Reservations 94

Chapter 10: Entertaining Diversions 97
Finding Entertainment Events Near Home . . . and Away! 98
Obtaining Listings 99
    Television 100
    Movies 101
Participating in Net Events 101
Taking Virtual Tours 103
Playing Online Games 104

CliffsNotes Review 107
Multiple Choice Questions 107
Practical Practice Projects 109

Resource Center 111
Books 111
Internet 112
Search Engines 113

Index 117

INTRODUCTION

This CliffsNotes Guide will rev up your journey in finding what you want on the World Wide Web. If you have a computer, an Internet connection, and a Web browser such as Netscape or Internet Explorer — then you're ready to hunt down and retrieve information and services online.

Half the battle of finding what you want on the Web is simply knowing what's out there. The other half is collecting what you want without wasting time muddling through the ever-growing heap of Web sites that inevitably distract you. This book will help you tackle both challenges by providing you with efficient search strategies as well as tried-and-true sources for obtaining the most commonly sought after Web information. Regardless of whether you're wanting to research Russian recipes, locate a distant relative, analyze your stock portfolio, or book a cruise, *CliffNotes Finding What You Want on the Web* will streamline your online quests into productive experiences.

Why Do You Need This Book?

You don't want to waste time staring at your computer screen, or poring over a 500-page guide book to understand how to find stuff on the Web. Like your fellow CliffsNotes brethren, you want a quick and easy way to learn the most important stuff you really need to know ("Just the facts, ma'am") — and *fast*. If you can answer "Yes" to any of these questions, then you're a prime Cliffs candidate:

- Do you need to learn about finding online information fast?

- Do you need to know some speedy, simple ways to weed from the Web only the pages and files you actually want?

2 CliffsNotes Finding What You Want on the Web

- Do you want to read the latest news headlines online to avoid buying papers at the newsstand or turning on CNN?

- Do you want to keep constant watch over your stock portfolio without calling your broker every ten minutes?

- Do you want to avoid battling mall crowds by shopping for birthday or anniversary presents online?

Then *CliffsNotes Finding What You Want on the Web* is for YOU!

How to Use This Book

You're the boss here. You get to decide how to use this book. You can read it cover to cover; use it as a hands-on tutorial; or just scan for the information you need and shelve it for later use. As a frequent CliffsNotes user myself, I'll share with you a few ways I recommend you search for your topic(s).

- Use the index in the back of the book to find what you're looking for.

- Locate your topic in the Table of Contents in the front of the book.

- Read the In This Chapter list at the beginning of each chapter.

- Look for additional resources in the CliffsNotes Resource Center.

- Or, flip through the book looking for your topic in the chapter subheadings since the material is arranged in a logical, task-oriented way.

Also, to speed your quest in finding important information in the book, we've placed icons next to the text. Here is a description of the icons you'll find in the book:

Introduction   3

The Warning icon alerts you to something that could be dangerous or that you should avoid.

The Tip icon clues you in to helpful hints and advice.

The Remember icon reminds you to make a mental note, because this text is worth keeping in mind.

Don't Miss Our Web Site

Keep up with the *changing* world of Web searching by visiting the CliffsNotes Web site at www.cliffsnotes.com. Here's what you find:

- Interactive tools that are fun and informative.
- Links to interesting Web sites.
- Additional resources to help you continue your learning.

At www.cliffsnotes.com, you can even register for a new feature called CliffsNotes Daily, which offers you newsletters on a variety of topics, delivered right to your e-mail inbox each business day.

If you haven't yet discovered the Internet and are wondering how to get online, pick up CliffsNotes *Getting On the Internet*, new from CliffsNotes. You'll learn just what you need to make your online connection quickly and easily. See you at www.cliffsnotes.com!

CHAPTER 1
GETTING STARTED

IN THIS CHAPTER

- Planning your search
- Working with a Web browser
- Sizing up available search tools

Never before has a single repository of information and services existed like the World Wide Web. The explosion of the Web has made it so that you literally now have available almost any item, idea, or contact you could possibly want to obtain.

With only a computer, an online connection, and the right software you can tap into a world's supply of libraries, public records, malls, and people. But do you have the "right software" for finding what you want? And are you really aware of the incredible range of offerings available on the Web? Most importantly, do you know how to locate what you're looking for, without wasting time clicking around aimlessly? This chapter helps you gets started on making your time online the most efficient and productive possible.

Planning Your Search

Some Web users love spending leisurely hours ambling through Web pages the same way some people love strolling through library stacks or the mall. However, if you're like me, you don't have time to waste: You want to go online, hunt down the bounty, and be done with it. To be an efficient finder, you need to know what's on the Web and how to make a beeline for just that.

Knowing what's available online

If you can read it, see it, or hear it — and it has even one redeeming scrap of interest for someone on the planet — then it's probably posted on the Web. Here's a summary of some of the key things that many Web users — including you — may be looking for:

- **Specific publication titles:** Books and magazines are frequently posted online. You can read or copy many of them in their entirety. Other pubs offer abstracts or summaries and provide subscription or ordering information telling you how to obtain the entire document.

- **The latest news:** While the hard-copy version is only available in early, morning, and late editions, you can use the Web to stay on top of breaking news headlines around the world. Many stories are accompanied by photos and video clips that you can see online long before they appear in print or on TV.

- **Everything posted about a certain subject:** Like a subject catalog at the library, you can check out all online information available on any topic you choose. Be forewarned that general subjects like "cats" will yield significantly more Web pages than specific ones like "ocelot kittens."

- **Specific Web sites:** You've probably already noticed the trend toward companies, organizations, and individuals including their Web addresses on business cards, billboards, and even commercials. Knowing specific addresses lets you instantly access their associated Web sites to learn more about who they are and what they offer.

- **Contact information for peopleand places:** Instead of calling directory assistance or skimming the yellow pages to find phone numbers and addresses, you can use a variety of online lookup sites to locate contact information worldwide. You can also find e-mail addresses, maps of the vicinity where the person or place is located, and more!

- **Ways to communicate with other people:** From e-mail to instant messaging, chat rooms, message boards, and even videoconferencing, the Web provides a wide variety of mechanisms for you to dialogue with others. You can talk with people you know and also find new friends (or loves!) with similar interests.

- **Reference materials:** The days of buying a set of encyclopedias from the door-to-door salesman are gone. Now you can find on the Web not only the entire A-Z collection, but also other references such as thesauri, famous quotes, media libraries, scientific field guides, and dictionaries in multiple languages.

- **Downloadable software:** As Web users obtain faster modems, it's becoming more practical to distribute increasingly larger software files online. You can get cool screen savers, try-before-you-buy demos, games, and inexpensive shareware programs all through the Web.

- **Government records and resources:** Every level of government is migrating its publicly available files to the Web, from home purchase records recorded in the city of Topeka to solar data obtained by NASA satellites. Get your "dot gov" here!

- **Online stores where you can shop:** Catalog shoppingis evolving to the next level as stores migrate their merchandise to "online malls" — and shoppers revel in the savings of cost, time, and parking frustration. With the Web and a credit card, your holiday shopping can be accomplished in a snap. The only thing you can't do? Try it on.

- **Investment information and services:** Novice and expert money managers will both benefit from the veritable treasure trove of Web-based investment materials now available. Banking, stock trading, business research, and many other services are now capable of being conducted online, eliminating costly time delays and "middle men" like brokers.

- **Classes:** Nontraditional learners such as business professionals and stay-at-home parents have long lamented the difficulties of making it to rigidly scheduled on-campus classes. But many schools and universities are now offering "distance learning" that make it easy for Web users to participate in online courses at home and at times that fit their busy lives.

- **Movie and music samples:** Why buy the DVD or CD without previewing it first? You can do precisely that by going online and checking out the latest media releases — sometimes long before the physical product hits the shelves.

- **Entertainment events:** Famous folks such as authors, singers and even the President are now performing and conducting public discussions via the Web. In many cases, you can not only see and hear the event as it happens online, but you can also submit a video or e-mail question to the presenter who may respond during the event.

The only information *not* available on the Web is information someone hasn't gotten around to posting (because it's either very old or very new) and information not made public for reasons of privacy or security (such as adoption records and nuclear missile launch codes.)

Is it free or is there a fee?

Most Web sites offer free access to users, viewing their information-sharing efforts as an inherent part of their outreach mission. Others sites stay afloat financially by sprinkling advertising from related companies throughout their pages. For example, many pregnancy and baby sites are chock full of ads for diapers, life insurance, and toys (like cool Curious George rocket lamps!) There is no fee for using these sites, unless you choose to buy something irresistible they happen to be selling.

Chapter 1: Getting Started 9

Only a small percentage of sites charge subscription or usage fees, especially when they provide unique services like assembling and organizing large volumes of information or posting online rapidly-changing information that's effort-intensive to track. One such subscription site, shown in Figure 1-1, is Classmates.com where you can locate and communicate with long, lost high school friends.

Figure 1-1:   It costs a small fee to obtain contact information for old friends at the Classmates.com (`www.classmates.com`) site.

Finding, not just surfing

Ever notice how hard it is to resist those impulse items placed at the checkout counter in the grocery store? You may not have gone to the store to get the Butterfinger, but you reach for it anyway. Key to finding what you want on the Web is not getting caught up in the eye-candy that litters most Web pages and distracts you from your finding mission.

Turning away from Web diversions may not be as easy as you think. The more you use certain Web tools to find what you want, the better they learn your specific interests and the more effectively they tailor pages to appeal to you. For example, using a personalized interface at the Yahoo! Web site, you may be presented with the latest headlines and ads relating to a favorite hobby of yours ... such as fitness. But if the reason you're online in the first place is to research an SUV purchase, you could easily kill minutes — or hours — perusing unrelated exercise items. Avoid getting off task by staying focused on finding the task you defined before sitting down at the computer.

I found it! Now where exactly is it?

Every page you look at on the Web is identified by a special *address* that tells you exactly where the page is located. The address or *URL* (universal resource locator) is important, because it's your way of knowing where you are on the Web. The URL of any page you view is always visible as you work online. (**See** "Navigating a browser window" for more details.)

When you finally find what you're looking for online, you can return to the same location instantly simply by typing in the URL. Alternatively, you can record the location — or *bookmark* — any URL you want to remember and return to that site later on simply by recalling the bookmark. (See "Bookmarking sites" for more details.)

Pick a Browser, Any Browser

Thescreens you view while ferreting out information on the Web are displayed using special software called a *browser*. Many Web users employ one of two main browsers, one called Netscape Navigator and the other called Internet Explorer. The use of either browser is free of charge, and one or the other is usually included in the setup materials from your chosen *Internet Service Provider (ISP)*. Alternatively, if you are using a service such as America Online or CompuServe 2000 as your ISP, the browser you use is probably one unique to that service. Regardless, all browsers look similar and share many common features, so it's up to you and your personal preference to choose which one you want to use.

Navigating a browser window

The browser provides you a simple interface window with areas for locating, viewing, and bookmarking Web sites. Working with a Web browser is just a matter of knowing how to use each area. Figure 1-2 shows the Internet Explorer browser.

Figure 1-2: The Internet Explorer browser viewing the main PBS Web site.

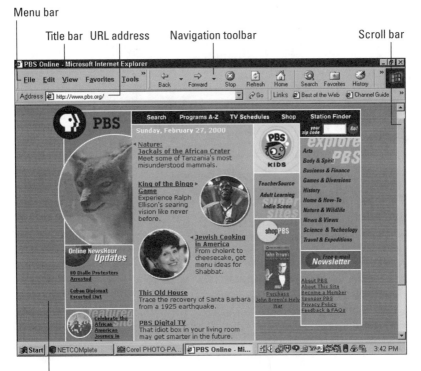

Table 1-1 points out each important area you can use in the browser.

Table 1-1: Areas of a Web Browser

Area	What's There	What It Does
Title Bar	Name of the current Web site	Informs you where you are on the Web
Menu bar	Browser management options	Allows you to print pages, change the size of text displayed, copy screens, and get help
Menu bar	F̲avorites (in Explorer); B̲ookmarks (in Netscape)	Allows you to record and revisit Web pages you want to remember (**See** Table 1-2 for details)
Nav toolbar	Back button	Returns you to the page previously viewed
	Search button	Opens a window or page where you can search the Web
Address (in Explorer) Location (in Netscape)	Web address	Tells you the exact location of the current page
Scroll bar	Vertical bar between two arrows	Allows you to look up and down the current page by moving the bar
Web page	Page matching the current URL	Presents the text, graphics, and other information located at that address in the large window

That little search button

A quick and easy way to start finding items of interest on the Web is to use the built-in search function that is part of your browser. Here's how:

   1. Press the Search button on the Navigation toolbar of your browser.

      Performing this action causes a new page (in Navigator) or a new window (in Explorer) to open where you can initiate your search.

   2. In the empty search box, type a word or phrase you want to search for.

   3. Press the Go Get It! button (in Navigator) or the Search button (in Explorer).

A list of Web sites that matches your chosen search word or phrase appears. Each site name is shown as a *hyperlink*, which means you can click it to open that particular Web site.

Scrolling over a hyperlink with the mouse causes the arrow pointer to become a hand ... that's how you know you've found a hyperlink!

Bookmarking sites

Finding Web pages that yield just the information you're looking for can sometimes be time consuming, so you don't want to retrace the entire search-and-retrieve process to revisit favorite finds. The solution? Like dog-earring a page in your current Michael Crichton novel, simply bookmark any Web page you want to return to. Table 1-2 shows you how, depending on your choice of browser:

Table 1-2: Recording and Revisiting Bookmarks (Favorites)

Action	In Netscape Navigator	In Internet Explorer
Recording a bookmark	From the Menu bar, choose Communicator➪ Bookmarks➪ Add Bookmark (Ctrl+D)	From the Menu bar, choose Favorites➪ Add to Favorites
Revisiting a bookmark	From the Menu bar, choose Communicator➪ Bookmarks and click your bookmark from the list that appears	From the Menu bar, choose Favorites and click your bookmark from the list that appears

In much the same way that people relocate from one house to another, URLs (Web addresses) often change. Unfortunately, unlike people who move, URLs don't always leave forwarding addresses. Pages you bookmark may no longer be valid when you try to revisit the bookmarks at later dates.

Gathering Your Search Tools

Much of your time spent scouring the Web will involve your use of two key types of tools: search engines and Web directories. There are lots of engines and lots of directories available online, and you can access all of them through your Web browser. Each tool type assists you in a unique way to help find information and services on the Web, so it's important to understand the distinction between how they operate.

Search engines

Like the mechanical device it implies, a search engine is a humanless machine that executes a search function on the pages that comprise the Web. Several search engines are available, some of them better than others at locating the information you want.

To operate a search engine, you must type a word or phrase into a search box (these words are called keywords) and then initiate the search. For example, you might type in the keyword "Prince" to locate information on the Artist Formerly Known As. . . . The engine then looks at every Web page it knows about and informs you of the pages containing your keywords. The pages are usually presented as a list, with the best matches at the top. Chapter 3 shows you how to employ savvy search strategies to use these engines to your best advantage.

Web directories

Web directories differ from search engines both in their construction and purpose. Directories gather related Web sites into groups and subgroups and name these increasingly specific groupings according to their contents — for example, **Entertainment**, **Music, Artists**, and **Prince**. Directory groupings are presented as hyperlinks, which you can then click to retrieve a listing of relevant Web sites. Because directories are typically created by real, live human beings, the Web sites they list tend to be less haphazard and provide more accurate matches than those retrieved by search engines.

Like search engines, there are lots of directories for you to use, and we'll explore the most productive ones in Chapter 2.

CHAPTER 2
LOCATING INFORMATION WITH WEB DIRECTORIES

IN THIS CHAPTER

- Browsing the Web with directories
- Strategies for pinpointing the sites you want
- Trying out a popular directory

Some of the most helpful navigation aids for finding what you want online are *Web directories*. Similar in form to a computer-based "yellow pages for the Web," directories arrange millions of Web sites into general *categories* and more specific *subcategories*. The beauty of this organization is that you don't have to know exactly what you're looking to find it in a Web directory. You need only start with a broad idea of the subject matter you want to explore — say, Recreation or Society & Culture — then begin to focus your finding efforts as you dig deeper down through the subcategories. The end result of using directories to find information online is a list of hyperlinked Web sites addressing the specific content you seek.

Deciding When to Use a Directory

The decision to use a Web directory is motivated by the same decision to use a restaurant menu: insufficient knowledge about all your options. You use a food menu anytime you want to eat at a restaurant, but don't know what food items are available. Similarly, you use a Web directory anytime you want to locate sites on the Web, but don't know exactly what those sites are.

Chapter 2: Locating Information with Web Directories

Perusing a directory (or a menu) to locate information you want is a process known as *browsing*. You start browsing by accessing a directory site such as Yahoo! (www.yahoo.com), shown in Figure 2-1, and looking at the general or *top-level* categories into which it organizes Web sites. Directories typically offer between 10 and 20 top-level categories, presented in a central location on their home page. From here, you decide where the subject matter you seek might logically reside and click the hyperlink for that category. For example, you would probably reason that Web sites you want to track down on hiking through America's national parks could be reached by selecting the Recreation category. (And you would be right!)

You may have to scroll down the page to view categories toward the bottom of the list.

Knowing What's Listed — and What's Not

Browsing is especially useful when you want to find sites on subject matter that other Web users may be interested in, too. That's because directory sites are usually built by real people. The more popular the subject matter, the more likely it is that someone building the directory has found a site — or been told about one — that they recommended for inclusion in one of the categories.

So if you're looking for some incredibly obscure tidbit of information, you will achieve greater success in finding what you want by searching the Web (see Chapter 3).

Around one million new pages of information are added to the Web every day, including many sites that sit online for a while before anyone gets around to reviewing and including them a directory. If you're looking for new information sites, search, don't browse.

18 CliffsNotes Finding What You Want on the Web

Figure 2-1: Yahoo! and other directories provide broad categories where you can begin browsing the Web.

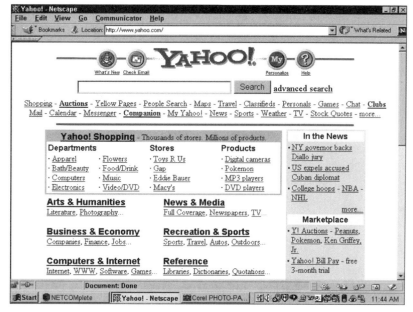

Working through the Hierarchies

Browsing a directory to find Web sites involves moving downward or *drilling down* through the directory's hierarchy of categories. Drilling down requires only that you make increasingly narrow choices to find what you want. You drill down from the most general (top-level) category through successively deeper subcategories (lower levels) until you reach the bottom where the Web sites are located. Web site names are listed as hyperlinks, which you can click to access the associated sites.

You can compare a restaurant menu and a Web directory by looking at the hierarchical steps you work through to accomplish two (seemingly unrelated) processes: eating a snack and finding a Web site!

Chapter 2: Locating Information with Web Directories

Table 2-1: The Drilling Down Process

Action	At a Restaurant	On the Web
Visit directory site	Drive to Marie Callendar's	Access Lycos
Look at site directory	Peruse menu	View Lycos categories
Choose top-level	Select desserts	Select Recreation category
Choose lower-level	Select pies	Select Outdoors category
Choose specific item	Order cherry pie	Click Adventure Living Web site
Consume item	Eat cherry pie	Review Adventure Living Web site content

Unlike a restaurant, the Web allows you to change course at any time. If you don't like the direction of your browsing, you can always click the back button to return to the page previously visited!

Using the Directories

Say that you spy a weird glow in the night sky and decide you want to investigate the notion of little green men visiting earth from outer space. You go online, open your Web browser, and realize you have no idea what specific Web sites contain content you seek. No problem! Just summon a directory and begin browsing through its categories. You can use a number of great directories, but one of the most popular (and my personal favorite) is Yahoo!

Yahoo!

The Yahoo! directory site (www.yahoo.com) provides 14 top-level categories where you can begin hunting for information online. Every Web site contained in the Yahoo!

directory lies within one of these top-level categories. Yahoo! also lists hyperlinks for some of the most frequently accessed lower levels directly below each top-level category. For example, the top-level category of Science lists the lower-level categories of Animals, Astronomy, and Engineering.

Be aware that the frequently accessed lower-level categories listed with the Yahoo! top-levels are not necessarily second-level categories. What they do represent are the largest and most popular lower-level categories in each top-level category.

Clicking on a hyperlink of any top-level category opens a new page listing all available second-level categories for that category. Figure 2-2 shows the second-level page that results for the top-level of Science. Notice that each second-level category is accompanied by a number in parentheses indicating how many third-level categories it contains. You can click on any second-level category hyperlink to display these even more specific third-level categories.

Continue clicking subcategory hyperlinks to drill down the Yahoo! hierarchy and find Web sites you want. From the second-level of Science, for example, you might click Astronomy to see even more specific lower levels as well as a list of general astronomy Web sites addressing that subject matter. You can then click on the hyperlink name of any of these Web sites to summon the site and read the information it has posted online.

Yahoo! usually begins listing specific Web sites at the third-level, and continues listing sites in the appropriate subcategories as you move lower and lower.

Keep track of where you are located within the Yahoo! categories using the hierarchy indicator in the upper left-hand corner of the currently displayed Web page. For example, Figure 2-3 shows that you are located in the third-level category of Paranormal Phenomena within the second-level category of <u>Alternative</u> within the top-level category of <u>Science</u> within the Yahoo! directory (<u>Home</u>

Figure 2-2: Second-level categories of the top-level category Science.

Figure 2-3: Look in the upper-left corner of the directory to determine where you are in the categories.

Every Web site accessible through Yahoo! is located somewhere deep down in the lower levels of the 14 top-level categories. If a Web site is listed in Yahoo!, regardless of the subject matter, its location is described by a carefully thought out sequence of increasingly specific categories. Here are two examples to demonstrate the thinking you need to employ when looking for sites of interest:

- Summer vacation is just around the corner, and you plan on spending it touring from coast to coast, riding the nation's most outrageous rollercoasters. Map out your plan by browsing: <u>Home</u> > <u>Entertainment</u> > <u>Amusement and Theme Parks</u> > <u>Roller Coasters</u>

- You invent a miracle device for retrieving lost socks from the netherland of the dryer. Discover how to patent your invention by browsing <u>Home</u> > <u>Government</u> > <u>Law</u> > <u>Intellectual Property</u> > <u>Government Agencies</u> > <u>United States Patent and Trademark Office</u>@

Keep in mind that often more than one browse sequence will route you to the same information. That's because Yahoo! cross-references information that falls into multiple categories. The "@" symbol lets you know that you're accessing a lower-level category that's being cross-referenced from it's actual "home" somewhere else in Yahoo!

Here's a final note to keep in mind when using Yahoo! The folks who perform the work of listing sites in the directory follow three simple principles for categorizing sites. Yahoo!'s three organizing principles for sites are

- Sites are cross-referenced from all likely browsing pathways

- Business and nonbusiness sites are distinguished at the top-level

- Regional and nonregional sites are distinguished at the top-level

Knowing these rules can help you streamline your browsing activities and minimize time wasted tracking down dead ends.

Other free offerings

The list of directory sites grows every day, a fact that benefits you as you go about finding goodies on the Web. Remember that very popular Web sites will be listed in most directories, but more obscure and more recently posted sites will only appear in a few directories — or possibly none at all. But because access to and use of most directories is free, you may find it helpful to try out several directories and see what they turn up. (See the Resource Center for a listing of suggested directory sites.)

Proprietary offerings

If you're using an Internet Service Provider such as America Online (AOL) or CompuServe 2000, you probably already know that your browser gives you access to special, proprietary information and online services that only members using your ISP can access!

Nonusers of your ISP can still access a host of information made available for free use by anyone on the Web, just not 100 percent of the good stuff you're paying for. To check out the free areas of CompuServe 2000, point your browser to www.compuserve.com, and to access AOL's open areas, point to www.aol.com.

CHAPTER 3
SEARCHING STRATEGICALLY WITH SEARCH ENGINES

IN THIS CHAPTER

- Developing and executing a search
- Using search results to find Web sites
- Trying out some popular search engines

Sometimes browsing is not the most time-efficient way to look for Web sites addressing the content you seek. In many instances — occasions when you want to locate very precise information quickly — you'll instead want to employ a *searching* approach to identifying hard-target matches. The searching process involves summoning a special Web site, called a *search engine*, and providing that engine with the specific information it must look for among the millions of sites on the Web. The engine uses software called a *robot* or *crawler*, which scours the Web and presents you with a list of possible matches for your request. After reviewing the matches, you may find one or more Web sites that provides exactly the information you want — or you may choose to refine and redo your search by employing new search criteria.

Deciding When to Use a Search Engine

Searching is especially useful under certain circumstances summarized in this checklist:

Chapter 3: Searching Strategically with Search Engines

- You don't have the energy or time to figure out where a topic you want to find might be located within the hierarchy of a directory's categories.

- You can guess that the Web sites you seek may not be popular enough to be listed in the categories of a directory.

- You want the most comprehensive listing of all possible sites addressing your subject matter.

- The information you want is precise and involves a number of limiting criteria. (For example, "Summertime square dancing events held in Sioux City, Iowa.")

- The information you want may be considered obscure.

- The information you want is very new.

Using a search engine for any of these reasons will achieve greater success than attempting to browse a directory because the search engine is not limited to the small number of sites categorized by real people. For better or worse, search engine robots provide you a run of the entire Web.

You should know that although search engines are capable of returning a remarkable number of close matches for your search requests, they aren't miracle workers. They sometimes include irrelevant sites, and they sometimes miss dead-on matches. Search engines aren't nearly as smart as you . . . yet!

Guessing Intelligently at URLs

One occasion when you shouldn't bother to search at all is when you can guess the URL (remember, that's the Web address!) of a Web site. For example, if you want to check out the latest casual attire, you may want to go to the Gap Web site to see what they have to offer. If you browse in Yahoo! (www.yahoo.com), you'll have to follow this pathway to reach your destination: Home > Business and Economy >

26 CliffsNotes Finding What You Want on the Web

Companies > Apparel > Labels > Gap. If you search in Infoseek (infoseek.go.com), you'll find not only the Web site you want (see Figure 3-1) but also some other off-target sites containing the word "Gap"— namely Gap-Toothed and Gender Gap. But since you know you are specifically looking for the Gap, the fastest way to get to that Web site is to guess at its URL and type it directly into the address or location area of your browser.

Figure 3-1: Venturing an intelligent URL guess may save you time sifting through these irrelevant search results.

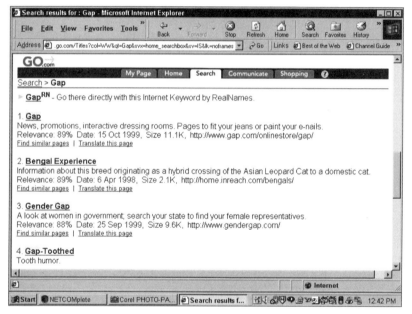

Here's a little formula you can use to make an intelligent URL guess:

URL = www.sitename.topleveldomain

Where . . .   *www* stands for World Wide Web

Chapter 3: Searching Strategically with Search Engines

sitename the company, organization, or product you seek

topleveldomain is a two or three-letter suffix of the site's top-level domain

If you're scratching your head wondering, "What's a top-level domain?" don't fret. A *top-level domain* is simply a special tag that classifies the Web site by its purpose. Table 3-1 shows you the six top-level domain names (excluding country codes), and you should commit them to memory to boost your success in guessing at URLs:

Table 3-1: Top-Level Domain Name Translations to Assist URL Guesses

Domain Name	Stands For	What It Means	Example
com	company of all types	U.S. Businesses	`www.nabisco.com`
edu	education	U.S. Schools, universities, educational institutions	`www.stanford.edu`
gov	government	U.S. Government all levels, from local to federal	`www.nasa.gov` at
mil	military	U.S. Military branches	`www.navy.mil`
net	network	Online networks, such as ISPs	`www.gte.net`
org	organization	Not-for-profit organizations	`www.girlscouts.org`
fr, jp, uk,...	country code that foreign	Site resides in uk country	`www.parliament.`

Guessing at a site name for The Gap would probably lead you to www.gap.com — a correct guess! What Web site would you guess represents the online presence of United Way? Bearing in mind that it's a nonprofit group, you might guess www.unitedway.org, and you would be right. You should also note that sites representing entities with multiple-word names either use the entity's full name without spaces, abbreviate the name, or use only the name's initials. For example, the Borders Web site is www.borders.com, while the Department of Energy site is www.doe.gov.

From Andorra (ad) to Japan (jp) to Zimbabwe (zw), every Internet-wired country in the world possesses its own two-letter domain name extension. For a complete list of country codes, check out www.ics.uci.edu/pub/Websoft/wwwstat/country-does.txt.

Choosing a Search Engine

Most of the major search engines use comparable techniques for helping you find information online. They crawl the Web to read what's online; they create an index of all the Web pages they find; and they match your search requests with everything they have cataloged in their respective indexes. The engines repeat the crawling and indexing over and over so that they catch the new sites being constantly added to the Web.

Besides relying on just a single search engine, you may also want to consider finding Web sites using a *metacrawler*, which sends your search request to several search engines all at once. The results of a metacrawler search are merged into a single, comprehensive listing of Web site results.

Even though there's tremendous similarity among all the major search engines, search-and-find "competitions" do reveal certain engines as winners or losers based on their ability to turn up on-target matches. Tables 3-2 and 3-3 give you a peek at the search engine medal winners you'll want to try. (See the Resource Center for a complete listing of search engines and metacrawlers.)

Table 3-2: Best Search Engine Picks

Engine Name	Web Address	Distinguishing Features
AltaVista	www.altavista.com	Contains one of the largest indexes. A favorite among researchers.
Ask Jeeves	www.askjeeves.com	Human-powered service. Uses everyday language. (See Figure 3-2.)
Excite	www.excite.com	Contains mid-sized index and non-Web content such as sports scores.
HotBot	www.hotbot.com	Most frequent "gold medalist" for successful matches.
Infoseek (GO)	www.go.com	Possesses a unique search method and a human-compiled directory.
Lycos	www.lycos.com	Gives results from both its directory and Web crawling.
Yahoo!	www.yahoo.com	The Web's most popular service. Features directory and crawling.

CliffsNotes Finding What You Want on the Web

Figure 3-2: See what others are looking for at Ask Jeeves (www.askjeeves.com), an everyday-language search engine.

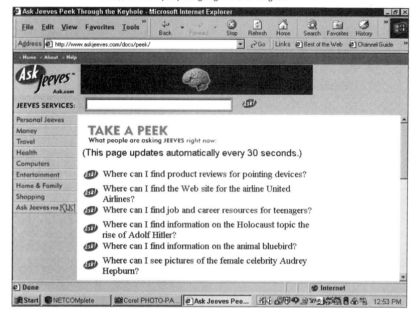

Table 3-3: Tried-and-True Metacrawlers

Metacrawler	Web Address	Distinguishing Features
Dogpile	www.dogpile.com	Customizable list of engines and directories.
Go2Net	www.go2net.com	Can present results in a single combined list.
Inference Find	www.infind.com	Groups related results by subject.

Tip

Check out www.searchenginewatch.com for the latest information on available search engines and metacrawlers.

Searching with a Keyword

A *keyword* is a word that a search engine looks for on the Web. To perform a search, you simply type a keyword into

Chapter 3: Searching Strategically with Search Engines   31

any engine's search box and press the Search button. Figure 3-3 shows a search in Go2Net for the keyword **Museum**. You can also type more than one keyword into a search box, although you need to know a few simple rules about how search engines handle multiple keywords (see "Refining your search," later in this chapter).

Each engine keeps a history of your previous keyword searches and informs you whenever you begin typing similar keywords for a new search. For example, Figure 3-3 shows that as I type the keyword **Museum**, the Go2Net metacrawler reminds me of previous keyword searches for **Museum of Natural History** and **Museum of Modern Art**. You can click any keyword in the drop-down list that appears and press Search to perform a Web search for those words.

Figure 3-3:   The search engine keeps a history of previous keyword searches.

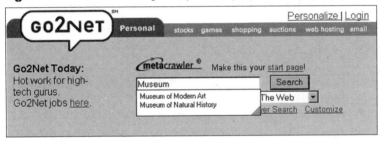

Reading search results

Clicking the Search button in a search box starts the process of locating all items in the engine's index that match your keywords. The search engine takes only a few seconds to present you a list of all the Web site matches or *hits* found. Matches are typically listed in order of *decreasing relevance*, meaning that the best hits are listed first, followed by less closely related hits as you go down the list.

Sometimes search hits are listed with a percentage: a percentage near 100% is a dead-on match and a percentage near 0% is a total miss. Search engines that also offer Web directories sometimes present search results in a special format. An engine/directory may first show hits within its own human-organized categories, followed by search results found from crawling the entire Web. You can see how this works in Figure 3-4, which shows the results for a Yahoo! search on Salsa dancing. Yahoo! retrieves three Category Matches (containing 53 Web sites) for Salsa dancing. Clicking the Web Pages hyperlink revs up the crawler and returns a list of nearly 8,000 Salsa dancing sites on the Web.

Search result listings — whether directory categories or Web sites — are presented as hyperlinks. You can click on any such link to access and explore the associated online information. After reviewing a link, you can easily return to the search results by clicking the Back button in your browser. Depending on how satisfied you are with the search results, you may choose to refine your search using techniques in the following section.

Figure 3-4: Yahoo! Search Results for a search on Salsa dancing.

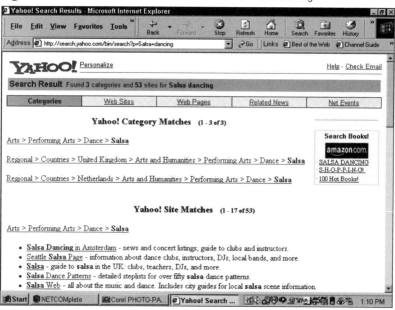

Chapter 3: Searching Strategically with Search Engines

Refining your search

Multiple keywords can be put together in special combinations to help you *refine*, or more specifically focus, your search. You will often find that you want to perform such refinements after reading the results of an initial search. If the results lead you to unsatisfactory Web site listings, you can redo the search using multiple keywords enclosed in quotation marks or connected with *Boolean operators* — the words AND, NOT, and OR. Just type your modified keywords into the engine's search box and press Search.

Here are some basic rules on using quotes and operators to refine your search:

- **Use quotes to enclose exact phrases that must be included in results.** "Indianapolis Colts" lists only sites about the Indianapolis Colts football team, avoiding sites about Indianapolis the city and sites about young horses. (**Note:** Many search engines presume quotes regardless of whether you actually type them.)

- **Precede keywords that must be included in results with AND.** Martian AND Marvin means that a site must contain the word Marvin to be listed. For example, you can use this strategy to find all sorts of Marvin the Martian sites! (**Note:** Depending on the search engine, you may be able to use the plus + symbol to represent AND.)

- **Precede keywords that must be excluded from results with NOT.** Martian NOT Marvin means that sites containing the word Marvin are not listed. Use this strategy to filter out Marvin the Martian sites when looking for sites on Martians. (**Note:** Depending on the search engine, you may be able to use the plus - symbol to represent NOT.)

- **Expand search results by connecting keywords with OR.** University OR college returns sites containing the word university and also sites containing the word college.

- **Combine multiple quotes and operators to significantly narrow search results.** For example, "San Francisco" AND ("bed and breakfast" OR hotel) returns sites about San Francisco bed and breakfast facilities and hotels.

You can also use the Advanced Search option offered by most search engines to further hone in on the sites you want. Advanced Search offers you easy ways to perform Boolean searches, constrain Web publication dates, and more. To explore this special feature, look in the special frame of the HotBot (www.hotbot.com) search engine.

CHAPTER 4
FINDING FILES AND DOWNLOADING DOCUMENTS

IN THIS CHAPTER

- Locating files on the Web
- Downloading and using files
- Cool places to find free software and other files

Who says that everyone searching online wants to find text information and read it off Web pages? You may have something a little glitzier in mind — like listening to digitized clips from Elton John's *Goodbye Yellow Brick Road* . . . downloading one of these little CliffsNotes . . . purchasing a shareware program to track your car maintenance records . . . or installing a funny screen saver.

The Web makes it possible for you to perform all these tasks and more by giving you access to computer *files* — programs or data collections that provide information to you or your computer. You can track down and use these files to add a whole new dimension to your computing experience — all you need to know is what file types are out there, and how to find them!

Common File Types

Files are categorized by their types, such as executable files or wave files (but not Rockford Files or X-Files). You can find out the file type by looking at its *extension* — sort of like a last name — that follows the period in the file's name.

CliffsNotes Finding What You Want on the Web

For example, **blackjack.exe** might be a little program that lets you play 21 on your desktop, while **byeyellow.wav** might be a song you can listen to through your speakers.

Table 4-1 gives you a quick summary of some of the major file types you'll work with:

Table 4-1: Computer Files by Type and Function

File Type	Extension	What It Represents
Acrobat	.pdf	Document with layout preserved. Open, read, and print using Acrobat Reader.
DLL	.dll	Provides functions or data to a Windows program.
Document	.doc	Document, such as a Word document
Excel	.xls	Excel spreadsheet
Executable	.exe	Application program
JPEG	.jpg	Commonly used graphics file format
MIDI	.mid	MIDI music file
MP3	.mp3	Movie or music file
PowerPoint	.ppt	PowerPoint presentation
Real Audio	.ra	Streaming audio file
Real Video	.rm	Streaming video file
Shockwave	.dcr	Shockwave file — enhances Web pages with multimedia such as animation
Wave	.wav	Digitally recorded sounds
Zipped	.zip	File which has been compressed with WinZip

Be forewarned about tinkering with DLL files unless you know what you're doing — you could damage your system!

Chapter 4: Finding Files and Downloading Documents   37

Locating Files

There's no hard and fast rule for finding files on the Web. You may discover that the technique for finding files with one search engine or directory is not exactly the same when you work with a different engine or directory. You may also find that certain Web sites are such excellent repositories of downloadable files, you don't need to go looking anywhere else! Here are a few tips for locating some popularly needed files:

- **Type the keyword file into the search box of a search engine.** This returns to you a list of Web sites that can serve as a starting point for acquiring the files you want. Some search engines may also make recommendations about more keywords you can search for to pinpoint specific file types. Other search engines, like HotBot, provide advanced search options that allow you to narrow your search to Web sites containing only file formats you specify, as shown in Figure 4-1.

Figure 4-1:   HotBot's advanced search options help locate the file types you designate.

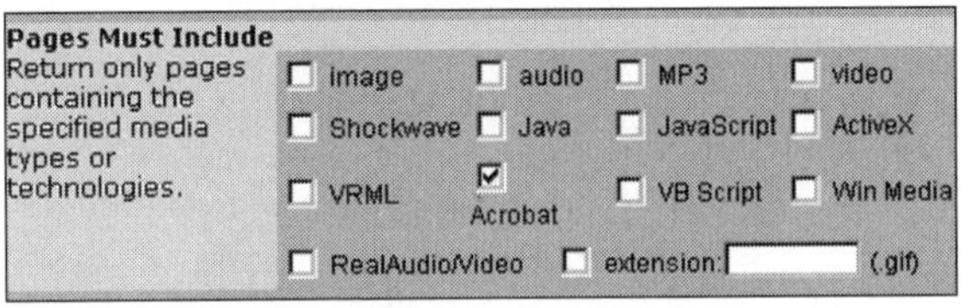

- **Browse to the software category in a directory.** In Yahoo!, you can follow the Home > Computers and Internet > Software path, which leads you to links for Freeware, Games, Screen Savers, System Utilities and other areas housing files. Similar pathways exist in all major directories.

- **Type a specific Web site URL into the Address or Location area of your browser.** Figure 4-2 shows the TopFile Web site (www.topfile.com), which maintains enormous archives offering thousands of free shareware, drivers, and dll files. (Don't know what those are? See Common File Types for details.)

Tip

You can also check the Resource Center at the back of this book for a list of Web sites featuring all types of free and nearly free files.

Figure 4-2: Web sites such as TopFile serve as file repositories with thousands of offerings.

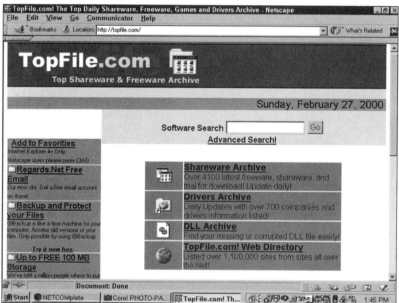

Downloading and Using Files

Once you locate a file, you may want to transfer it to your own computer so that you can use it. The transfer process, called *downloading*, takes anywhere from a few seconds to several minutes as the file is transmitted bit by bit to your computer. Once the entire file is downloaded, you can either

Chapter 4: Finding Files and Downloading Documents

install it or view (or listen to!) its contents, depending on its file type. Files you install are typically programs. Files you view or hear are typically data files such as Word documents, movies, or sound files.

Some files, specifically *streaming* media files like Real Audio and Real Video, are not downloaded to your computer at all. You view them or listen to them playing through the Web without actually transferring them to your computer.

Downloading a file varies somewhat based upon the Web site you visit, and the specific browser you are using. The basic procedure usually follows these simple steps, although don't be surprised if what you see on-screen differs from the description below (in that case, just follow along with the on-screen directions):

1. After locating a file you want to download, press the Download button or link.

   A dialog box may open asking you to choose where you want to save the downloaded file.

2. Press the Browse button to select a save folder and then press OK.

   If such a dialog box does not appear, the file may automatically be saved to your C drive in the Program Files folder.

3. During downloading, a dialog box appears indicating the transfer progress. If you want to stop the download, press the Cancel button.

   Figure 4-3 shows how this dialog box appears when transferring a freeware program from one of the premiere download sites, ZDNet (www.zdnet.com). This dialog box disappears when the download is finished. An icon or filename representing the file appears in the folder you selected in Step 2.

After the download completes, you can browse to the newly saved file and double-click its icon or filename to begin using it. If the file is a program, you are led through a procedure for installing the program; if the file is a document, it opens so that you can view its contents.

You can view a downloaded document only if your computer has an application program capable of opening and displaying the document's contents. For example, you'll probably need Microsoft Access — or a program that can translate Access files — to open and view a downloaded Access database document\.

Figure 4-3: Downloading spreadsheet freeware from the ZDNet Web site (www.zdnet.com).

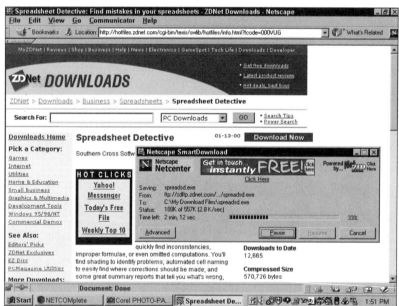

Getting Freeware

Freeware is exactly what it sounds like: free software. It provides you full-version educational programs, screen savers, business tools, and other files you can download and use free

Chapter 4: Finding Files and Downloading Documents

of charge. Some of the most popular freeware are files created by altruistic, my-stuff-is-your-stuff programmers who give away their cool creations via the Web. Other freeware takes the form of *Beta-version* software, files that product manufacturers are evaluating with real users (that means you) prior to releasing the final, for-pay product.

Because Beta software products are not "finished," you may encounter some *bugs*, or problems, when using them.

Contrary to what you might think, this freeware stuff isn't junk! You can often get much more than what you pay for ($0 in this case) with freeware, including items such as these:

- **PGPfone — Pretty Good Privacy Phone** (www.pgpi.org/products/nai/pgpfone) turns your computer into a secure telephone.

- **RealPlayer and RealJukebox** (www.real.com) play a huge assortment of live and prerecorded video, music and talk radio on your desktop. Beta-versions are often available which let you try out the latest and greatest features before they're commercially released.

- **Search for Extraterrestrial Intelligence Screen Saver** (setiathome.ssl.berkeley.edu) lets you help look for civilization beyond Earth by running an analysis of actual radio telescope data as your screen saver (think, *Contact*).

For specific guidance on finding freeware titles on the Web, see "Locating Files," earlier in this chapter.

Acquiring Cool Demos

Demonstration or *demo* files are try-before-you-buy software offerings you can download for free from the Web. Demos are basically pared-down samples of the full versions you receive when buying the actual software products. You can obtain thousands of demos on everything from games to home and family helpers. Sites such as ProgramFiles.com (`www.programfiles.com`) provide comprehensive lists and descriptions of available demos (see Figure 4-4), along with links to the sites where you can perform the downloads.

Figure 4-4: Try the Coach's Assistant demo for free! If you like what you see, you can buy the full version online.

Trying out these demo files is a great way to compare products and test whether you want to fork over the cash for the complete product. You can find demos available for downloading as follows:

- **Type the keyword demo into the search box of a search engine.** A list of Web sites appears that can serve as a starting point for acquiring demos you seek. If you are looking for a demo addressing a particular subject, be sure to include that subject in your search. For example, you can find demos of CD-ROMs on health by typing the keywords **demo AND health**.

- **Type the URL of the Web site for a software manufacturer who sells the product you want to try.** For example, Adobe sells fantastic — but pricey — software for developing multimedia and Web materials. Before buying an Adobe product, you can go to their Web site at www.adobe.com and download the product's demo version to test-drive its features.

Purchasing Shareware

Shareware is budget-priced software that costs more than freeware but less than commercially distributed products. You can download shareware from the Web in exactly the same way you obtain freeware and demos — but most likely you'll have to supply a credit card number (or pay up using some other means) to complete the transaction. Like all software offerings, shareware titles run the gamut from fun games to serious programming applications. The real beauty of shareware is that it's often the only way you can get unique or unusual files that are too obscure to be otherwise produced and distributed. For help in finding a huge assortment of shareware offerings online, see "Locating Files" earlier in this chapter.

CHAPTER 5
FINDING NEWS, WEATHER, AND SPORTS INFORMATION

IN THIS CHAPTER

- Getting the latest news online
- Watching the weather
- Following your favorite sports

Since the emergence of mass media, people have relied on newspapers, television, and radio to supply the latest information about occurrences in the world. These media have been the first to print daily temperature forecasts, broadcast images from the moon, and air the World Series play-by-play. But these traditional vehicles have a downside: They keep you informed according to their schedules, at times that don't necessarily match the occasions when you want to find out what's happening. I don't know about you, but I don't have time to watch the Weather Channel long enough to determine if I need a rain slicker for my afternoon business trip to San Francisco. And what diehard football fan wants to wait for the Monday paper to view the latest NFL stats? Enter the Web. By going online you can find out all the news, weather, and sports of interest to you — anytime, anywhere you want!

Digging Up the Daily News

Using the Web as your news source, you can transform not only how you see the news, but what kinds of news you view and which sources deliver it. Almost every major news provider has established a Web presence that rivals its

Chapter 5: Finding News, Weather, and Sports Information

original format of print, audio, or video. For example, you can now access the *Chicago Tribune* online at www.chicagotribune.com; National Public Radio at www.npr.com; and CBS News at www.cbsnews.com. You can even use the Web to soak in that compelling *National Enquirer* cover story or something a little more mundane like your hometown newspaper. You can do all these and more — if only you know where to look.

Personalizing a page with your favorite news sources

For those among you who enjoy sampling a variety of news sources, there's a clever tool you can use to gather the latest news according to your unique preferences. It's called a *personalized page,* and it appears on a single Web page custom-tailored daily just for you.

Personalized pages are offered free of charge by many search engine and directory sites. These pages require only that you register with the site so that it can issue you a user ID and password to keep track of your information preferences. One good site for creating and maintaining a personalized page is Excite. Follow these quick and easy steps to set up your page:

1. Access the Excite Web site at www.excite.com.

2. If you are new to Excite, press the New Members Sign Up hyperlink. If you are already an Excite Member, click the Sign In hyperlink. New members are asked to register before receiving a personalized page. The Excite Sign Up page asks you to complete a short registration form by typing the requested information in the empty boxes. This makes you a member so that hereafter you need only type your member name and password to sign in. Completing the Sign Up or Sign In form opens your personalized page.

3. At your personalized Excite page, press the Edit button in the My News area.

4. At the Personalize My News Categories! page (Figure 5-1), add a news category to your personalized page by clicking the category in the Select topics area and pressing the Add button. Your category appears in the Selected topics area. Repeat this step for each category you want included on your personalized page.

Pressing the Advanced Personalization button at the Personalize My News Categories page provides additional customization choices such as the number of headlines displayed per topic.

5. Remove any selected category by clicking the category in the Selected topics area and pressing the Remove button.

6. Press the Finish button. Your personal page now displays the news headlines from the categories you selected.

Bookmark your personalized page (see Chapter 1 for details) or make it your home page for easy access when you go online.

Reading your hometown newspaper online

A great way to read your local newspaper — and save the environment in the process — is to forego the rolled-up hardcopy and read the news online. Reading your hometown newspaper online is available so long as you live in a fairly sizeable city with sufficient newspaper circulation to support a companion Web site. That means cities such as Houston, Seattle (see Figure 5-2), and Nashville — although even smaller towns are in the process of migrating their papers to the Web. (See the Resource Center for a list of other online newspapers.)

Chapter 5: Finding News, Weather, and Sports Information

Figure 5-1: Choose the categories of news headlines you want displayed on your personal page.

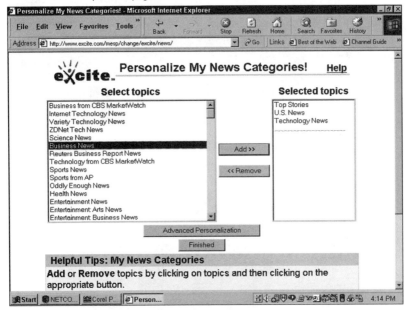

Besides reading sections from today's paper, you can also retrieve archived editions, usually up to a year old. Additionally, employing the search feature of an online paper allows you to quickly scan for specific articles or subjects you may be researching.

Reading the want ads and other classifieds can be expedited by performing a search of your online newspaper. Just type a keyword such as "Accountant" into the search box and let the computer do the work for you.

Getting alerts as headlines break

News isn't news unless its up-to-the-minute. So be the first one to know what's up — not by staying glued to your personalized news page — but by having the news sources contact you with breaking headlines. The Yahoo! Web site

48 CliffsNotes Finding What You Want on the Web

(www.yahoo.com) makes available two free tools for just that purpose: Yahoo! Messenger and Yahoo! News Ticker.

Figure 5-2: Read the Seattle Times online at www.seattletimes.com.

- **Yahoo! Messenger** is a small window that sits on your desktop and displays constantly updated news. Messenger runs as a separate program you can download from messenger.yahoo.com and then install on your computer.

  The first time you run Messenger, you'll need to register as a Yahoo! user by pressing the Get a Yahoo! ID button at the Messenger Login dialog box. You can later customize Messenger's headline sources by pressing the Messenger News tab and then the Edit button.

  Using Messenger is simply a matter of letting the program run while you work at your computer. Update headlines by choosing Login➪Refresh from the Messenger menu bar. Click any intriguing headline to

Chapter 5: Finding News, Weather, and Sports Information

open a Web page where you can read the complete story. For details on working with Yahoo! Messenger, see *CliffsNotes Exploring the Internet with Yahoo!* by IDG Books Worldwide, Inc.

- **Yahoo! News Ticker** is a compact information banner that sits quietly in the Taskbar at the bottom of your computer screen, scrolling current news as shown in Figure 5-3. It presents the same information as Yahoo! Messenger, but in a perpetually visible linear format. You must download and install a separate program from `my.yahoo.com/ticker.html` to begin using the Ticker. This page also provides a Need Help? area that you can access to find answers to commonly asked questions about using the Ticker.

Figure 5-3: Yahoo! News Ticker scrolls the latest news in a space-saving desktop banner.

Besides news, both Yahoo! Messenger and Yahoo! News Ticker can show the latest stock quotes sports scores and other information according to choices you make at `my.yahoo.com`. See Chapter 8 to see how Messenger appears on your desktop.

Thumbing through online magazines

Getting your weekly fill of *People, Glamour, Consumer Reports, Time, Good Housekeeping, Parenting, PC Week,* and other magazines can be an expensive, time-intensive undertaking. Why not consider the alternative of reading online versions of your favorite magazines instead?

Online magazines like *Newsweek* (Figure 5-4) are not duplicates of their print versions, but rather complementary companions for each weekly or monthly issue. They provide some of the same content, but focus mainly on presenting shorter articles of similar themes, updated more frequently than the regular publication. Web mags also offer you interactive options not available in print, such as the ability to voice your opinion on a story by participating in an online poll. The only drawback to opting for online magazines is foregoing having something distracting to read on the treadmill at the gym! (See the Resource Center for a list of online magazines.)

Figure 5-4: Newsweek and other magazaines publish distinct Web counterparts.

Tracking the Weather

Weather Web sites offer a tremendously useful service to anyone living outside of Los Angeles where the climate is always sunny and 78 degrees. While you once relied on your TV meteorologist to predict tomorrow's weather, you can now tap an assortment of scientifically supercharged sites to show you everything from temperature to pollen count, at any location on the planet.

Chapter 5: Finding News, Weather, and Sports Information 51

One site worth examining is AccuWeather (www.accuweather.com), which provides current conditions and predictions for your local area, region, the entire nation, and the world. As shown in Figure 5-5, you can view data in a variety of numerical and visual formats including Doppler radar and even satellite maps.

Figure 5-5: Rain or shine, you'll always know what weather to expect after visiting the AccuWeather site.

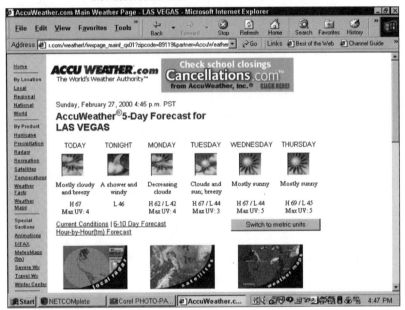

AccuWeather also provides special services, such as listings of school closures due to inclement conditions, and weather reports sent directly to your e-mail account. You can even choose to receive official National Weather Service warnings for tornados, flash floods, and other severe weather via your personal pager. (See the Resource Center for a list of weather sites.)

Consider adding a customized weather module to your personal Web page to keep tabs on conditions in your local area.

Following Sports

Staying on top of all the latest sporting events can be difficult, even for an athletics enthusiast. Who really has time to follow every football, basketball, hockey, tennis, and auto racing competition that takes place? Well, *you* do, because the Web now makes it possible for you to catch all the hot sports action from the comfort of your computer station — all you have to supply is the big pretzel. From full coverage sites such as ABC Sports (www.abcsports.com) to league sites like the WNBA (www.wnba.com), you'll never again miss another thrill of victory or agony of defeat.

Personalizing a page with your favorite teams

Using a procedure similar to the one you learned in this chapter's "Personalizing a page with your favorite news sources," you can create a custom Web page that lists recent sports news and scores. Virtually all sites offering personalized pages reserve a portion of your page for sports information, as shown in Figure 5-6. It's up to you to choose which events and which teams you want included in that area. Here's how to customize the My Sports area of the personalized Excite page you created earlier:

Figure 5-6: Track team performance and game activity on your personalized page.

Chapter 5: Finding News, Weather, and Sports Information

1. Access the Excite Web site at www.excite.com.

2. If your personalized page does not appear, press the Sign In hyperlink. Type your member name and password to sign in. This opens your personalized page.

3. At your personalized Excite page, press the Edit button in the My Sports area.

4. At the Personalize My Sports Teams! page, click a league hyperlink in any category.

    Available categories consist of Football, Baseball, Basketball, Soccer, and Hockey.

5. At the Choose your favorite page, add a team to your personalized page by clicking its name in the Select teams area and pressing the Add button. Your team appears in the Selected teams area. Repeat this step for each team you want included on your personalized page. Alternatively, you can hold down the Shift or Ctrl key to select multiple teams.

6. Remove any selected team by clicking its name in the Selected teams area and pressing the Remove button.

7. Press the Finished button.

8. Repeat Steps 4-7 until you have added all the leagues and teams you want.

9. Press the Save button. Your personal page now displays the sports scores for the teams you selected.

Pressing any team hyperlink in your My Sports area opens a Web page providing details on the team, including player information, current standings, and game schedules. Pressing any score link in My Sports opens a Web page showing a play-by-play game rundown for that game.

Watching and hearing streaming sportscasts

Using one of the Web's many streaming media players (see "Watching and hearing streaming newscasts" in this chapter), you can enjoy your favorite game action without turning on a TV or radio. For example, sports sites such as ESPN (www.espn.com) provide broadcast audio coverage so that you can listen to almost any game in real-time on your computer. That's a tremendous plus when local radio stations don't cover away games in events like baseball.

Other sites, including the one owned by the NFL (www.nfl.com) offer short, post-game video clips, such as the one shown in Figure 5-7, featuring highlights from hot match-ups throughout the season. The quality isn't great, and the viewing window is tiny, but it's certainly better than foregoing any footage at all! The only thing you generally won't find on the sports sites, however, is live video of games-in-progress. (Pay-Per-View still has the market cornered on that. . . .)

Figure 5-7: "View or listen to your favorite players as they punt, bunt, and dribble."

CHAPTER 6
TRACKING DOWN AND INTERACTING WITH PEOPLE

IN THIS CHAPTER

- Finding people you know . . . or want to know
- Corresponding with others via e-mail and instant messaging
- Socializing in the online community

Have you ever thought about what it's like trying to find and communicate with people without the Internet? You may use the white pages to find phone numbers and addresses for local folks you want to contact, and you may call directory assistance to track down such information for people outside your stomping grounds. Then you probably dial up or mail letters to let those individuals know the information you want to tell them — or to ask them about things you're trying to find out. The whole process is time consuming and not always fruitful, depending on how lucky you are with reaching people who bother to write or call you back!

Using the Web, you can not only find contact information for people, but also use quick and easy online tools to connect with them. It takes only a few seconds to type and send your mom an e-mail or your boss an instant message — and they can just as easily send a reply to your note. ("Yes, son, I'll wire $1,000 today," or, "No, you can't have tomorrow off!") And because Web-based interaction is less formal than traditional correspondence, you'll find it a simple task to find and converse with people you've never met, about virtually any topic. Without paying long-distance charges or international postage, you can use the Web to talk to people half a planet away about your common interest in scuba diving or just to chat about the day's news.

Locating Phone Numbers, Addresses, and More with White Pages

The fact that "The new phone book's here, the new phone book's here!" may have caused great joy for Steve Martin in *The Jerk*, but when it comes to locating contact information, you'll revel in the Web's mightier (although not weightier) resources. That's because the Web offers a number of sites that provide conglomerate *white pages*, pulled together from hundreds of phone books for cities coast to coast.

White pages offer not just phone numbers and mailing addresses, but in many cases they can also yield e-mail addresses and other contact information such as maps of the area where a person lives. Many times you can find white page listings for persons whose names you know — even when you don't know what cities they live in. Figure 6-1 shows how you can use partial information to find a phone number or e-mail address using the Switchboard Web site located at www.switchboard.com. The less information you type, the more white page listings you receive. For example, you can perform a lookup when you know just a last name, as in, "He said his name was Mr. Martinez." Such a lookup provides you listings of all persons in the white pages with that last name. (In this case, probably a very long list!)

Many online white pages also let you add yourself to their listings if you find you've been left out of their contents. They also typically allow you to supply your e-mail address if you choose. (See the Resource Center for additional white page Web sites.)

Chapter 6: Tracking Down and Interacting with People 57

 Trying to find high school classmates and sweethearts? Try www.classmates.com site. You can list current contact and personal information about yourself and obtain e-mails from friends you haven't seen in years!

 Some white pages allow you to create and view personal information pages so that Web users can "meet" each other online. One such site is Yahoo!'s People Search (people.yahoo.com), which links to Yahoo! Profiles (profiles.yahoo.com). There, you can build a personal profile for yourself (including biographical data, photos, and contact information) and read those posted by other people.

Figure 6-1: Switchboard (www.switchboard.com) assists you in finding people's phone numbers and e-mail addresses.

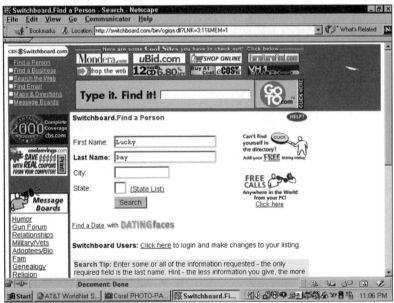

Getting Information from Others via E-mail

One of the best ways to find what you want — on the Web or otherwise — is simply to ask someone. And what better way to ask someone than to send them an e-mail; you don't have to pay long-distance phone charges, and they can respond to you at their convenience. Plus, with resources like Web white pages (see "Locating Phone Numbers, Addresses, and More with White Pages," earlier in this chapter), you greatly increase your chances of finding the e-mail address of precisely the folks you want to reach.

Additionally, you can now get an e-mail account, a *free* e-mail account, from any number of online providers. And because these e-mail accounts are maintained on the Web, you can send and receive e-mail from any Internet-wired computer that lets you access the Web site of your chosen provider. (Translation: You don't have to be at your home computer to use e-mail!)

Setting up an e-mail account: a Hotmail example

One popular e-mail provider is Microsoft Network's Hotmail, located at www.hotmail.com. Hotmail is free and easy to use, but you can find many other excellent e-mail providers as well so be sure to glance at the Resource Center for more choices. If you're a new user, you can get a Hotmail account by following these steps:

1. Open the Hotmail Web site by typing www.hotmail.com in the Location or Address area of your browser and pressing Enter or Return.

2. At the Hotmail home page, click the Sign up now! hyperlink in the New user? Area.

3. At the MSN Hotmail Terms of Service page, read the agreement, scroll to the bottom, and click the I Accept button.

4. At the Hotmail Registration page, type in the empty boxes to complete the Profile Information and Account Information areas and then click the Sign Up button.

Chapter 6: Tracking Down and Interacting with People

5. At the Sign Up Successful page, grab pen and paper and write down your new Hotmail e-mail address. For example, mine is `camille_mccue@hotmail.com`, and I use this address when sending or receiving e-mail messages.

6. Click the Continue at Hotmail button.

You are now a registered Hotmail user, and you are returned to the Hotmail home page.

Signing into your Hotmail account

As a registered Hotmail user, follow these steps to begin using e-mail:

1. Open the Hotmail Web site by typing `www.hotmail.com` in the Location or Address area of your browser and pressing Enter or Return.

2. At the Hotmail home page, type your Sign-In Name (the part of your e-mail address before the @hotmail.com) and your Password in the empty boxes and then click the Sign In button. You're now signed in to your Hotmail account.

Can't recall your password during sign-in? Click the Forgot Your Password? link for assistance in Hotmail. Other e-mail services offer similar help.

Note: The first time you sign-in to your new Hotmail account, you see a WebCourier FREE Subscriptions page. At this page, click to check the boxes of the subscription titles that interest you and then click the Continue button. At the WebCourier Subscription Confirmation page, click Done. News and features from your selected subscriptions will be sent as e-mail messages to the Inbox of your Hotmail account.

60 CliffsNotes Finding What You Want on the Web

At your Hotmail Inbox page, shown in Figure 6-2, you see a summary of all e-mail messages currently residing in your Inbox. You also see six tabs — Inbox, Compose, Addresses, Folders, Options and Help — which you can click to access different features of your e-mail account. Table 6-1 describes the function of each e-mail feature.

Figure 6-2: The Hotmail Inbox shows e-mail you have received. Click any message to read its contents.

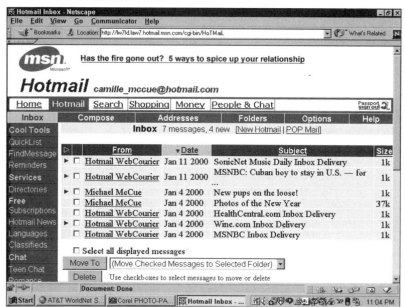

Table 6-1   Hotmail Features

Tab	Action
Inbox	Shows the contents of the Inbox folder (new mail and messages not moved to other folders).
Compose	Opens a form where you can type and send an e-mail message.
Addresses	Opens an address book where you can add e-mail contacts.
Folders	Shows existing mail folders (Inbox, Sent Messages, Drafts, Trash Can) and allows you to create and name new mail folders.

Chapter 6: Tracking Down and Interacting with People   61

Tab	Action
Options	Opens menu where you can change your account information, filter out junk e-mail, and route messages from other accounts to Hotmail.
Help	Opens the help menu for the area of Hotmail you are currently using.

Using and managing your Hotmail account

Here are some of the most commonly performed activities you perform while signed into Hotmail:

- **Read your e-mail messages:** Click the Inbox tab and then click the hyperlinked title of any message to read it.

- **Reply to an e-mail message:** In an open message, click the Reply button (or the Reply All button if you want to reply to everyone who received the same message).

- **Forward a received message to someone else:** In an open message, click the Forward button. Type the intended recipient's e-mail address or a Nickname from your Address Book in the To: empty box.

- **Create and send a new message:** Click the Compose tab. Type the recipient's e-mail address or a Nickname from your Address Book in the To: empty box. Type your message in the large blank box and then click the Send button.

- **Add someone to your Address Book:** Click the Addresses tab. In the Individuals area, press the Create New hyperlink. At the Create Individual Nickname page, type the person's Nickname and his or her E-mail Address in the empty boxes (you can complete the other boxes if you wish). Click OK.

- **Delete an e-mail message:** Click the Inbox tab. Click to check the box next to any message you want removed and then click the Delete button. Deleted messages are moved to the Trash Can folder, which is emptied by Hotmail several times a week.

- **Create a new mail folder:** Click the Folders tab and then click the Create New hyperlink. At the Create Folder page, type a New Folder Name in the empty box and then click OK.

- **Read messages in a mail folder:** Click the Folders tab and then click the Folder name hyperlink you want to view.

- **Move a message to a different folder:** Click to check the box next to the message you want to move. Select the folder where you want to move the message from the drop-down menu beside the Move To button and then press Move To.

You can, of course, perform many other tasks in your Hotmail account. Don't forget to click the Help tab to get assistance in executing those tasks.

Joining Common Interest Clubs

Want to get together with buddies to swap ideas on a common interest? Then Yahoo! Clubs may offer just the perfect gathering forum you need. Yahoo! Clubs (clubs.yahoo.com) is a collection of online meeting places where people with similar hobbies or unique leisure pursuits can congregate to exchange their ideas and ask advice. You need only obtain a Yahoo! ID to join any Yahoo! Club.

Figure 6-3 shows you an example of the Saltwater Aquarium club, but you have hundreds of club choices, which explore everything from Senior issues to Spirituality to Spying. And

Chapter 6: Tracking Down and Interacting with People   63

if you don't see a club that matches your interests, you can start your own by pressing the Help hyperlink in the Create a Club area at the bottom of the Clubs home page.

You cannot post messages to a club unless you are a member of that particular club. However, you can read messages posted at most clubs to determine whether you want to join up.

If you haven't signed in to Yahoo!, you'll need to do so before posting messages to your clubs.

Figure 6-3:   Joining a Yahoo! Club allows you to communicate online with others who share your special interest.

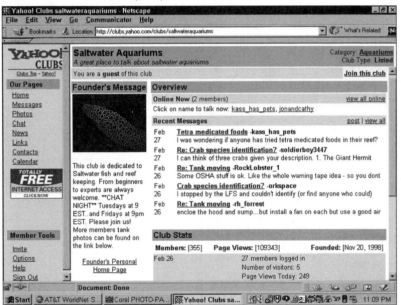

Using Instant Messaging

Remember sitting next to a lab partner in biology class, hastily scribbling little notes on a scrap of paper, passing it back and forth during a lecture as secretively as possible? Then welcome to the electronic version of note passing for the new millennium: instant messaging. *Instant messaging*

(IM) is basically a way of exchanging e-mail or voice messages in real time. You don't have to wait for the messages to arrive in your e-mail box — you see or hear them as they are sent, without any delay. It's quick, it's easy, and you can get started simply by downloading an IM program from the Web.

A number of Web sites offer you free IM programs including AOL (`www.aol.com`), MSN (`messenger.msn.com`), and Yahoo! (`messenger.yahoo.com`). An overwhelming IM favorite, though, is the internationally popular ICQ ("I seek you") program located at `www.icq.com`. With several million downloads to its credit, ICQ not only allows you to instantly message with friends and colleagues, but also to find a random person online, anywhere in the world, and strike up a conversation. Figure 6-4 shows an example of ICQ in action.

Figure 6-4: ICQ's Find Random Chat Partner button opens this dialog box where you can find other users to IM.

Chapter 6: Tracking Down and Interacting with People

AOL Instant Messenger comes with recent versions of Netscape, so check to see whether you already have a shortcut to this IM located on your desktop. If so, then the program is installed, and you don't have to perform any additional downloading!

People you want to communicate with via IM must use the same IM service as you — or a compatible service that's capable of exchanging notes with your messenger.

Downloading and installing an IM: an ICQ example

To use an IM program, you (and all the people you want to message with) must download it from the Web. Here's how to download ICQ:

1. Access the ICQ home page (www.icq.com) and click the "Get ICQ for Free" button.

2. At the Download ICQ page, scroll down and click the download hyperlink appropriate for your computer.

You can choose from ICQ for Windows 95/98/NT4, ICQ for 68K Mac, ICQ for PowerPC, as well as others.

Note: Several more pages may appear prior to starting the actual download. At each new page that appears, click the download hyperlink or button for ICQ.

3. When the download begins and the File Download dialog box appears, click the Run This Program From Its Current Location radio button and click OK.

Your computer starts downloading ICQ and shows you a dialog box indicating download progress until complete. The installation process then begins automatically.

4. Follow the steps in the ICQ installation dialog boxes until the Installing dialog box informs you that the process is complete.

Using ICQ

To run the installed ICQ program, follow these steps:

1. In Windows, select Start➪Programs➪Icq➪ICQ. On a Mac, just double-click the ICQ program icon in the folder where you installed ICQ. The first time you use the program, an ICQ Registration Wizard starts, leading you through several screens you must complete to set up and use ICQ on your computer.

2. Follow the Registration Wizard screens, typing the requested information in the empty boxes and clicking Next to advance to each subsequent screen. When your registration completes, you are provided an ICQ# that uniquely identifies you as an ICQ user.

    At the Location and Additional Details screen, type only the information you want to share in the empty boxes. Pressing the buttons (such as Personal and Language) summons additional dialog boxes where you can input specific details about your background and interests. Providing this information helps random ICQ users know a little about you — and helps you know a little about them (refer to Figure 6-4). This minimal information may help you decide whether to venture out, click the Send button, shown in Figure 6-5, and IM with an ICQ user you don't know.

3. Jot down your assigned ICQ#. You can use this number to access ICQ from any computer that has the program installed. From now on, for all subsequent times you start ICQ on your home machine, the ICQ window automatically opens so that you can immediately begin instant messaging.

When you're first starting to use ICQ, click the Instruction button in the ICQ window to open an ICQ help page in

Chapter 6: Tracking Down and Interacting with People

your Web browser. This help page offers a guided tour and a help index to assist you in become an active instant messenger quickly and painlessly!

Figure 6-5: Pressing Send instantly delivers this IM to the ICQ user located via Find Random Chat Partner.

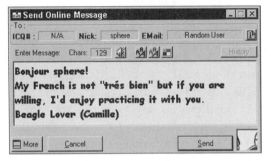

Chatting in Chat Rooms

Like riding on an elevator where you know no one yet can talk to anyone, online chat rooms provide you a unique meeting place for interacting with other Web users. And like all elevator rides, online chats involve a high turnover of individuals entering and exiting the elevator — er, chat room — resulting in somewhat trivial conversations taking place during the brief periods when people interact. Still, chat rooms have some redeeming value in that they allow you to eavesdrop on (and also contribute to) online conversations with other Web users who are expressing their most human thoughts, opinions, hopes, dreams . . . you get the idea.

Chat rooms are offered by many major directory providers such as Lycos (www.lycos.com), as well as specialty Web sites such as iVillage (www.ivillage.com), which features content of particular interest to women. Most chat sites actually offer several rooms segregated by the interests or common characteristics of the persons who might want to visit those rooms. For example, Lycos offers "TV Shows ER" and "The Political Agenda" chat rooms in its extensive lineup, while iVillage offers "Work From Home" and "Parenting" chat rooms. (See the Resource Center for a complete list of sites offering chat rooms.) The vast majority of chat rooms require you to register with the parent site to obtain access to the chats, although a few providers allow you to sign in and chat anonymously.

The best, most engaging chats are scheduled as structured, moderated Net events featuring a special guest (Rrrricky Martin!) or discussion about a narrowly defined subject (such as an impending Senate vote) with a specific start and end time. In this format, the chat evolves into more of a stimulating campus lecture or an energetic dinner party discussion. See Chapter 10 for more information on participating in Net Events conducted as chats.

CHAPTER 7
LOOKING IT UP — ONLINE LIBRARIES AND REFERENCE MATERIALS

IN THIS CHAPTER

- Accessing everyday reference tools: dictionaries, thesauri, encyclopedia, and atlases
- Digging into the Library of Congress
- Thumbing through Virtual Reference Collections

Doing research is a task that usually strikes fear into the hearts of third-graders and doctoral dissertation students alike. You know how difficult it can be to locate sources that *may* contain the information you seek, and you also know how frustrating it can be to actually *find* those sources available, sitting on their designated shelves ready for checkout or photocopying.

Now you can take care of all your research needs, both large and small, through the simple interface of the Web — and you do it using all the libraries of the world that have put their holdings online. You can find rhymes for your poetic musings, maps of the world, and access to the millions of documents housed at the Library of Congress. Many complete references are provided online, while others can be electronically ordered and sent via e-mail or U.S. mail.

70 CliffsNotes Finding What You Want on the Web

A quick and easy way to get started is simply to click the hyperlink for the top-level category of Reference in any major directory. There you'll find links to lower-level categories listing Web sites for thousands of almanacs, encyclopedias, handbooks, style guides, and more, as shown in Figure 7-1.

Figure 7-1: The Reference top-level category in AltaVista (www.altavista.com) connects you with a varied and complete assortment of research and reference tools.

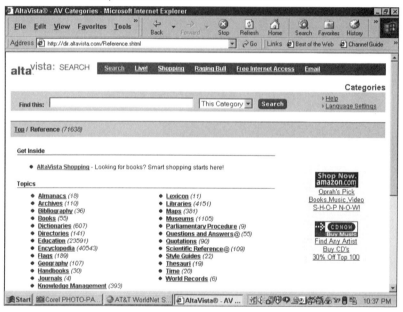

After exploring a lower-level category or Web site, you can return to the Reference top-level by pressing the back button in your browser. Additional information on working with Web directories is located in Chapter 2 and in the Resource Center.

Digging into Online Dictionaries and Thesauri

Need to find out whether that 85-point, game-winning word your Scrabble opponent just laid down is legitimate? Tired of repeatedly using the words "reinvent," "paradigm," and "infrastructure" in your presentations? Are you trying to track down the meaning of a term *d'art* in medicine, technology, or another specialized field? Then tap into an online dictionary or thesaurus to find new words and discover the meanings of those you don't know. Here are some of the great offerings you can get on the Web:

- **Cambridge International Dictionaries:** Search for dictionary meanings, including idioms, at www.cup.cam.ac.uk/elt/dictionary.

- **Foreign Language Dictionaries:** Link to 25 languages translators, from Afrikaans to Yiddish, at dir.yahoo.com/Reference/Dictionaries/Language/.

- **Lexical Freenet Connected Thesaurus:** Find connections between two words, similarly spelled words, and more by going to www.link.cs.cmu.edu/lexfn.

- **Merriam Webster Dictionary/Thesaurus:** Type a word to look up its meaning or locate synonyms by visiting www.m-w.com.

- **The Nonsensicon:** Use this dictionary of nonexistent words (remember Sniglets?), located at www.nonsensicon.com.

- **Subject Dictionaries:** Link to subject dictionaries such as law, medicine, music, and defense by visiting dir.yahoo.com/Reference/Dictionaries/Subject/.

- **WriteExpress Online Rhyming Dictionary:** Find rhymes on any syllable for a given word at www.writeexpress.com (see Figure 7-2). Great for writing songs and poems.

Figure 7-2: WriteExpress (www.writeexpress.com) gives you rhymes for any word you input.

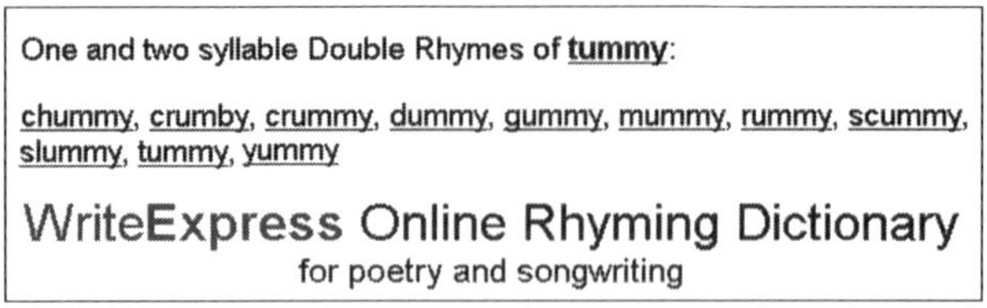

One and two syllable Double Rhymes of **tummy**:

chummy, crumby, crummy, dummy, gummy, mummy, rummy, scummy, slummy, tummy, yummy

WriteExpress Online Rhyming Dictionary
for poetry and songwriting

Retrieving Content from Encyclopedias, Maps, and Atlases

Gone are the days when you buy a hefty 26-volume hardcover encyclopedia set from the kindly door-to-door salesman. And although it may have warmed your heart to hear the crackling sound as you first bent a freshly bound spine, it's cheaper, faster, and a significant space-saver to find encyclopedic entries on the Web. Every major encyclopedia publisher has migrated its offerings to a digital delivery system, with much of the material available free of charge. Here are a handful of the best offerings.

- **Brittannica:** Type in any topic and press Find, or choose a subject from the Explore list at www.britannica.com.

- **Encarta:** Access 16,0000 reference articles, a world atlas, and searchable categories at encarta.msn.com, shown in Figure 7-3.

- **Encyberpedia:** Search numerous categories at this site, which has excellent atlas information. Located at www.encyberpedia.com/ency.htm.

Chapter 7: Looking It Up — Online Libraries and Reference Materials

- **Funk and Wagnalls:** Enjoy this unabridged encyclopedia loaded with multimedia flags, maps, and more by visiting www.funkandwagnalls.com. Updated monthly.

Figure 7-3: Encarta (encarta.msn.com) and other encyclopedic sites provide online access to articles and maps.

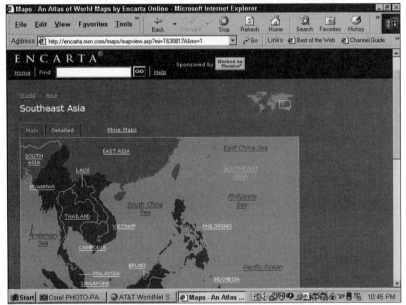

Getting Cool Clips from Media Libraries

For creating newsletters, presentations, and Web sites, you can find some fantastic (and free!) multimedia clips online. Need a Morse code sound effect? Some clip art? A few seconds of video from a classic flick? Then take a look at these sites.

- **A+ Art:** Link to sites providing free animations, buttons, backgrounds, and clip art at www.aplusart.com.

- **Hollywood.com:** Access photos, sounds, and videos from tons of films by going to www.hollywood.com/multimedia.

- **Microsoft Clip Gallery Live:** Download clip art, photos, sounds, and animations if you're a licensed Microsoft product users. Just visit `cgl.microsoft.com/clipgallerylive`.

Tip

Download most clips by right-clicking the clip's hyperlink and then selecting the Save as option in the menu that appears. For Clip Gallery Live, follow the special download directions provided at the site.

Visiting the Library of Congress

Located in Washington, D.C., the Library of Congress is the world's largest library, dedicated to fulfilling its self-proclaimed mission to, "Boldly go where no one has . . ." Oops! Wrong mission. The Library of Congress' mission is to "Sustain and preserve a universal collection of knowledge and creativity for future generations." It houses more than 100 million items, from presidential papers to Magellan's maps to early motion pictures and recent digital media. Just try browsing *those* stacks!

Well, you don't have to fly to the nation's capitol and walk the aisles to peruse the Library's holdings. All you have to do is go online, type `lcWeb.loc.gov` into the Address or Location area of your browser and press Enter or Return. And voilà! You are instantly transported to the Web-based Library of Congress, where you can explore its vast Collections, access the Copyright Office and even survey its virtual Exhibitions.

To being finding Library holdings, click the Search The Catalog hyperlink on the main page and then click the Use The Online Catalog Button on the page that appears. This summons the Library of Congress Online Catalog page (shown in Figure 7-4) which provides you with several search options for locating what you want. Whether you're a researcher, publisher, or educator, you'll likely to find what you need at this information-packed Web site!

Chapter 7: Looking It Up — Online Libraries and Reference Materials   **75**

Figure 7-4:   The Online Catalog of the Library of Congress Web site (lcweb.loc.gov) boasts access to the world's largest library — and numerous other interconnected libraries around the world.

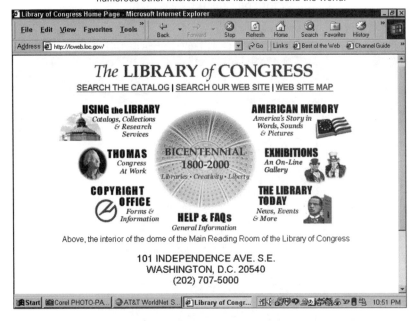

Finding Information on Everything with Virtual Reference Collections

If you're a fan of one-stop shopping, you'll love the concept of the Virtual Reference Collection. Why? Because such a collection provides a single access point for looking up the types of reference information you need most frequently. One of the best collections is the Internet Public Library (www.ipl.org/ref), shown in Figure 7-5.

Here, you find links to information on subject categories by clicking a subject heading such as Health & Medical Sciences. (Think of these subjects as encyclopedia headings.) You can also click the Reference heading to access links to Almanacs, Biographies, Calendars, Demographics, Genealogy, and many other usual reference tools. And if you just can't find

76 CliffsNotes Finding What You Want on the Web

what you're looking for, click the <u>Ask a Question</u> sign on the librarian's desk, fill out the Reference Form, and wait quietly (sssshhhh!) for your answer via e-mail.

Figure 7-5: The Internet Public Library (www.ipl.org/ref) offers a collection of links to popluar reference sites in one location.

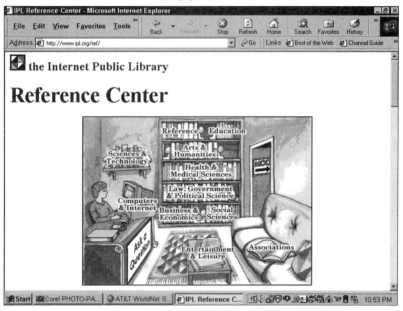

CHAPTER 8
GETTING DOWN TO BUSINESS . . . AND GOVERNMENT INFORMATION

IN THIS CHAPTER

- Finding business and financial information
- Managing your money online
- Locating government resources

Whether you're a meticulous money manager who budgets wisely and balances his checkbook or an investor wannabe with no more than piggy-bank savings, the Web can help you find everything you need to become financially savvy and secure. You can locate business news, financial calculation tools, tax forms, and constantly updated stock information. And when you're ready, you can take the plunge and start investing online, monitor your money's growth, and even eliminate mundane tasks like writing checks by migrating to online bill-paying.

The Web also offers ever-increasing access to government sites that yield local, state, and federal resources you want to find. For example, sites such as Federal Bureau of Investigation (www.fbi.gov) give you the lowdown on the Bureau's duties and activities (those it can reveal!). The only government material you won't find online is classified information: They could tell you, but then they'd have to kill you!

Tracking Down Business and Financial Sites

You can find a vast collection of business and financial resources on the Web, and you can access the sites that house that information by using either of these two methods:

- **Go to any major directory site, select the top-level category of Business, and drill down through the subcategories to find the sites you want.** Every directory features some variation of Business in its top-level categories, so you'll have luck using this strategy regardless of the specific directory you choose. For example, in Yahoo! (www.yahoo.com), clicking the top-level category of Business and Economy leads you to second-level categories, which include Business Libraries, Companies, Finance and Investment, Real Estate, and Taxes. AltaVista's (www.altavista.com) top-level Business and Finance category leads you to lower level categories for Accounting, E-Commerce, Financial Services, International Business and Trade, Resources, Small Business, Venture Capital, and many others. For assistance in working with directories, see Chapter 2.

- **Type the address of a specific business or financial site into the Address or Location area of your browser and press Enter or Return.** You can explore several excellent sites, and each one boasts its own unique strengths. To get started, check out the Money Web site at www.money.com and look around its categories of Markets, Investing, Real Estate, Insurance, Retirement, Autos, Taxes, and Tools. Notice that the Tools category offers special calculators for computing a variety of financial information, including "How Much Life Insurance Do I Need?" (see Figure 8-1), "How Fast Will my Nest Egg Grow?," and "The Relocation Wizard." (See the Resource Center for more recommended business and financial sites.)

Chapter 8: Getting Down to Business . . . and Government Information

Figure 8-1: Money (www.money.com) gives you free, easy-to-use calculators for computing and graphing all sorts of financial data.

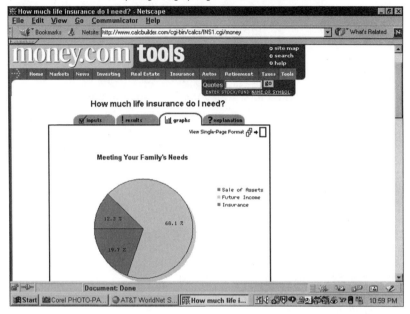

Running a small business can be a *tricky* business, especially when your company is in its infancy. You need communications and promotional tools to generate business and earn money, but you can't acquire the tools you need because you're strapped for cash! Yahoo! Small Business (small-business.yahoo.com) can help by providing a collection of handy tools you need to get your business going. Small Business gives you links to pages addressing how to open your business on the Web, sell your wares through Yahoo!, conference call online, and track packages through the Web. It also offers informational stores on handling taxes, legal issues, office supplies, human resources, and more!

Following News about Money

A simple way to monitor what's happening in the world of money is to follow the business, economics, and financial news posted on the Web. Even better, you can have the latest money news headlines delivered directly to you on a free personal Web page that you custom tailor to your specific needs. Take a look a Figure 8-2 for an example of how a module featuring breaking money news appears on a personal page constructed in Excite (www.excite.com). Chapter 5 gives the details on setting up a customized page in any of the major directory Web sites.

Figure 8-2:   Customize a Web page to deliver money news from sources you select.

Investing Online

If stocks, bonds, and mutual funds pique your interest (no pun intended), then the Web has some nifty investment opportunities for you. Although many directory sites allow you to set up free portfolios and monitor their performance, the number of sites that allow you to buy and sell online is much more limited — and it'll cost you to use them.

Chapter 8: Getting Down to Business ... and Government Information

Monitoring stocks with Yahoo! Messenger

You can hold your finger on the pulse of the stock market by keeping a small information window — Yahoo! Messenger — constantly running on your desktop. That's because Messenger shows continuously updated stock quotes from customized portfolios you set up for free in Yahoo! (see Figure 8-3). In fact, using Messenger requires only that you let the program run while you work at your computer. No more reading the little numbers in the newspaper!

Figure 8-3: Stay on top of your stock portfolio by having Yahoo! Messenger send you continuous updates.

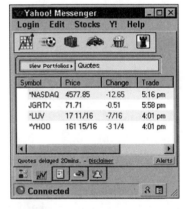

Messenger doesn't allow you to *trade* stocks, but it does allow you to monitor their performance.

To use Messenger, you must first download the program from `messenger.yahoo.com` and then install it on your computer. The first time you run Messenger, you'll need to register as a Yahoo! user by pressing the Get a Yahoo! ID button at the Messenger Login dialog box. You can then set up portfolios as follows:

1. On the Messenger, press the Stocks tab and choose Stocks⇨Edit My Portfolios from the Messenger Menu bar.

2. Update stock quotes by choosing Login➪Refresh from the Messenger menu bar and double-click any intriguing quote to open a Web page where you can read the complete information.

   3. Set stock alerts (such as when an upper or lower limit you designate is tripped) by choosing Edit➪Preferences from the Messenger Menu bar, choosing the Stocks tab in the dialog box that appears, and making your selections.

For details on working with Yahoo! Messenger, see CliffsNotes *Exploring the Internet with Yahoo!* by IDG Books Worldwide.

Going solo with Fidelity

One for-pay site that allows you to actually execute investment transactions on the Web is Fidelity (`www.fidelity.com`) — a comprehensive site that also provides sound guidance about your options along the way. Here, you can research the history and performance of any stock, bond, or fund and their parent companies; trade when it's convenient for you; and keep tabs on your account activities with a variety of helpful tabular and graphical analysis tools. Fidelity online allows you to effectively get rid of your broker by putting you in charge of the trading and money management tasks you previously had him perform. (See the Resource Center for additional sites featuring online trading.)

Accessing Government Sites

The "G" in G-Men must stand for "Gee, let's put it on the Web!" considering the tremendous volume of information now posted online by government sites. From the CIA, NASA, and the Internal Revenue Service (see Figure 8-4) to your hometown city council, virtually every branch of

Chapter 8: Getting Down to Business . . . and Government Information

government at every level is making its public documents available for access via the Web. You can find tax forms, congressional transcripts, and local ordinances for vaccinating your pets — anything dealing with government activities.

Figure 8-4: The IRS (`www.irs.gov`) and other government sites provide public access to their documents and activities.

Table 8-1 summarizes how to access the various levels of government Web sites you want to find. Table 8-2 some examples of specific information you can find at U.S. government sites. (I list additional site names and addresses in the Resource Center.)

Table 8-1: Finding Government Web Sites

Type	Site Format	Representative Site	Site Address
Federal branch	www.branch-initials.gov	The Central Intelligence Agency	www.cia.gov

(continued)

Table 8-1: Finding Government Web Sites (continued)

Type	Site Format	Representative Site	Site Address
State branch	www.state gov.state-initials	The Kansas State Government	www.state.ks.us
County branch	www.co.county-name.state-initials.us	Clark County, Nevada	www.co.clark.nv.us
City branch	www.ci.city-name.state-initials.us	The City of Detroit	www.ci.detroit.mi.us

Table 8-2: Examples of Information Available on U.S. Government Web Sites

Site	Site Address	What's Available
America's Job Bank,	www.ajb.dni.us	Millions of online resumes and job listings, along with Department of Labor guidance in obtaining employment.
Department of Education's Gateway to Educational Materials	www.thegateway.org	Lesson plans by grade level for teachers, home-schoolers.
Department of Energy	www.doe.gov	Tips for saving money by becoming more energy-efficient.
Department of Health	www.healthfinder.gov	Help on choosing health plans, doctors, treatments.and Human Service's Healthfinder service
Department of Housing	www.hud.gov	Homebuyer's kit, list of available HUD homes and approved and Urban Development HUD lenders.

Chapter 8: Getting Down to Business ... and Government Information

Site	Site address	What's available
Internal Revenue Service	www.irs.gov	Downloadable tax forms, tax tips, online filing!
Small Business Administration	www.sba.gov	Loans, assistance for women and minority-run businesses, plus a database of contracts available to them.

For additional examples beyond Table 8-2, check out "Twenty Things You Can Do and Learn On U.S. Government Web Sites" located at www.whitehouse.gov/WH/New/html/20-things.html.

CHAPTER 9
SHOPPING FOR PRODUCTS AND SERVICES

IN THIS CHAPTER

- Buying via the Web
- Selling merchandise online
- Reserving and purchasing travel

Online shopping offers more than just a good way to avoid the physical exhaustion of traveling from store to store and wasting time in the checkout line. For one thing, it gives you the ability to shop at a greater selection of stores than you could patronize practically. Did you realize that you can buy smoked oysters from Alaska, airlines tickets to Brazil, and a selection from Oprah's Book Club, all in a single session online? You can even comparison shop with newfound ease — after all, you don't have to "go" anywhere to get the best deal, you just have to return to the Web site with the cheapest prices.

Additionally, you can play the role of an e-barterer, selling items on the Web to potential buyers who can make you an offer online from anywhere in the world. Sort of like having a garage sale ... just without the garage!

Locating Goods for Sale

On the Web, you don't have to look at a mall map or in the yellow pages to see what stores are open for business. You just need to know a few handy tips for finding the goods you want to buy. Here are a few suggestions:

- **Type the URL of a specific store in the Address or Location area of your browser and press Enter or Return.** You may have seen an ad in a magazine or elsewhere that tells you this URL. An example is The Gap, which is located at www.gap.com.

- **Make an intelligent guess about the URL of a specific store site you want to access.** For example, if you want to look at new BMWs, you could guess that its Web site is located at www.bmw.com. Just type your guess in the Address or Location area of your browser and press Enter or Return. (See Chapter 3 for help on making intelligent URL guesses.)

- **Click the Shopping hyperlink on any major search engine or directory.** This opens a new page showing shopping options featured by your selected engine or directory. For example, clicking the Shopping hyperlink on the Microsoft Network home page (www.msn.com) opens MSN Shopping. The page provides links to featured stores and product categories where you can start browsing product lines such as Family and Pets or Gourmet. You can also enter a specific product name in the Search box and press Search to head directly for that item. (See the Resource Center for a listing of search engines and directories.)

- **Type the URL of an online shopping mall in the Address or Location area of your browser and press Enter or Return.** One you'll want to try is www.piiq.com as shown in Figure 9-1. This site offers hot shopping news along with a diverse collection of e-commerce Web sites. Just click any category's hyperlink and start making your selections. (See the Resource Center for an extensive listing of online shopping malls.)

88 CliffsNotes Finding What You Want on the Web

Figure 9-1: The piiq online mall lets you shop from your desktop.

Purchasing Products Online

Once you find an item you want you buy during your shopping excursion on the Web, it's usually a simple procedure to buy it. The process varies slightly depending on the specific sites you're visiting, but here are some general rules to follow for completing your online purchase through commercial sites:

1. For the item you wish to purchase, click the Add to Cart or Buy It button. This opens a Shopping Cart page, as shown in the eToys site of Figure 9-2, which lists all the items you have selected. The new item you have selected is added to the list along with its unit price.

2. At the Shopping Cart page, type the quantity of the item you want to purchase.

3. Compute the total item cost by pressing the Update Quantities button or hyperlink. If you have multiple items in your cart, the total cost of all items will be updated as well.

4. To remove an item from your cart, press the Remove button or hyperlink. The contents of your Shopping Cart are updated to reflect the change.

5. To continue shopping, press the Return to Shopping button. As you find new items you wish to purchase, repeat Steps 1-4 to adjust the items in your cart.

6. When you are finished shopping the site, press the Checkout button. A new page appears showing your final item list and costs. Also, this page usually informs you whether any items are discontinued or backordered.

7. If you wish to ship your selected items to multiple addresses, click the items you want to ship first and complete the ship-to form for the recipient. The form usually asks for the recipient's name, mailing address, and phone number. You may also be asked to provide a shipping priority, such as ground, two-day air, or overnight. Additional charges will be listed for each associated shipping priority.

8. Repeat Step 7 for the remaining items and shipping addresses.

9. At the billing information form, type the requested information in the blank boxes. You are typically asked for your name, billing address, phone number, e-mail address, credit card number, and expiration date. A confirmation page is displayed indicating the completion of your order. The page often includes a confirmation number you can refer to in the event of shipping problems or charge errors. It's a good idea to print out this form and keep it handy until you know that all deliveries are completed without incident.

Figure 9-2: Each shopping site provides a "cart" listing your selected items for purchase.

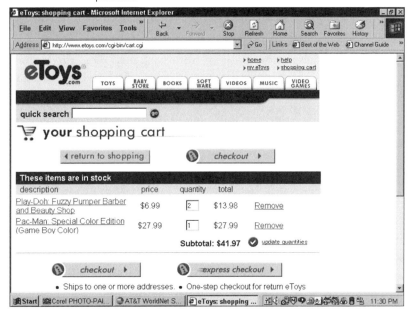

Shopping sites differ somewhat in their selection and checkout procedures, so don't be surprised to find variations in the preceding procedure.

Some sites do not inform you in product listings or during checkout that an item is discontinued or back-ordered. They may instead send you an e-mail regarding order status after you've already made your purchase. Be especially cautious about ordering and shipping gifts via e-commerce near the holidays due to heavy demand for popular items.

Sending an e-present at the last minute for a birthday or anniversary? You should know that sending flowers or balloons can be safer than sending e-gifts. That's because if your selected flower variety or balloon color is out-of-stock, a similar item can be easily substituted — thus guaranteeing a timely delivery. Shopping sites do not substitute e-gifts.

Buying and Selling via the Classifieds

Besides purchasing from commercial shopping sites, a great way to find what you want to buy is to snoop through online classifieds — especially when you're looking to acquire big-ticket preowned items like cars and homes. Using online classifieds is also an equally great way to let other people know about items that you want to sell. Just think about online classifieds as a countrywide version of the ads you see posted each week in your local Sunday paper.

You can access online classifieds by clicking the Classifieds hyperlink available on the home page of many search engines and directories. For example, clicking the Classifieds hyperlink on the Yahoo! home page (www.yahoo.com) opens Yahoo! Classifieds — one of the most comprehensive listings of Web-based ads available. At this page, you can click on category hyperlinks such as Air & Water Craft to read ads, as shown in Figure 9-3. Ad listings can also be narrowed to include only those geographic regions you specify by pressing the Change Location hyperlink. For example, you may choose to look at ads for the entire United States, all of Maryland, or just Baltimore.

If you are interested in purchasing an item found in a classified ad in Yahoo!, you can contact the seller by clicking the Reply to this ad hyperlink located at the end of the listing. (**Note:** Because Classified sites vary, the reply hyperlink may be named something else in other sites you peruse.) An e-mail form appears showing the To (the ad's lister) and Subject fields already completed. The From field (your e-mail address) may already be completed, or you may need to type in an address where you want the lister to respond. All that's left is for you to type a sentence expressing your interest in the ad in the Your Reply Here area. Click the Send Message button to deliver your message or click Cancel to discard it.

Figure 9-3: Each classified ad provides details and contact information about the sale item.

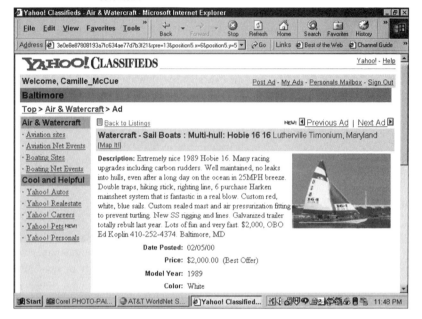

It pays to be diligent and check your e-mail on a regular basis ... you never know when a buyer will send a message stating he's ready to close the deal on an ad you've posted!

Participating in Online Auctions

Web-based auctions have become the hot new way to buy and sell one-of-a-kind items and antiques you just can't purchase in a store. From banjo wall clocks to rare Tunisian stamps, auction sites like eBay (www.ebay.com) are matching willing online bidders with the objects of their affection. (See the Resource Center for a listing of auction sites.)

eBay, like most online auction sites, consists of some key areas you need to know about in order to successfully bid, buy, and sell at auction:

Chapter 9: Shopping for Products and Services   93

- **Welcome new users:** This area helps you register as an eBay user and also explains the rules for participating in auctions and placing items up for bid.

- **Categories:** This area is divided into categories you can browse, such as <u>Antiques</u> and <u>Coins & Stamps</u>. Each category name is followed by the number of items up for bid in that category ... literally hundreds of thousands! Clicking an auction category leads to a list of hyperlinked subcategories, each of which lists all related auctions in progress, as shown in Figure 9-4. For each auction, you can see the name of the item, the price (the highest bid), how many bids have been placed, and the closing date and time. Clicking any hyperlinked item name opens a page that provides details about the item (including pictures and seller reliability ratings) and an area where you can add your bid to the auction.

- **Find it!:** In this area, you type an item you want to find in the What Are You Looking For? box and press the Find It! button to search for auctions featuring that item.

- **My eBay:** Clicking this hyperlink opens a page that gives you a handy summary of all items you're currently bidding on and the outcome of recently closed auctions in which you participated.

As with a traditional auction, it ain't over till the auctioneer yells "Sold!" If you absolutely must win a particular auction, monitor the bid history closely to stay one step ahead of your competition. Pay close attention to the auction's closing date and time to ensure you're victorious with the highest bid.

Figure 9-4: Bay offers online auctions where bidders can vie for unique items.

Making Travel Reservations

A major benefit of shopping online is the time and cost savings you realize when arranging travel. By avoiding the use of a travel agent, you waste no time talking on the phone, miss no potential vendor offering, and pay no overhead for services rendered. Even better, by taking travel reservations into your own hands, you can plan and purchase tickets whenever it's convenient for you — in the middle of the day or the middle of night.

Using Web-based travel services, you can arrange air, car, hotel, and even cruises with a few strokes of the keyboard. You may choose to make reservations at a specific site, for example at Hertz Rent-a-Car (www.hertz.com). Or you may opt for exploring all available offerings at a conglomerate travel site such as Preview Travel (www.preview travel.com), as shown in Figure 9-5. (See the Resource Center for a listing of travel reservation sites.)

Chapter 9: Shopping for Products and Services

Figure 9-5: Book air, rental car and hotel reservations with sites such as Preview Travel.

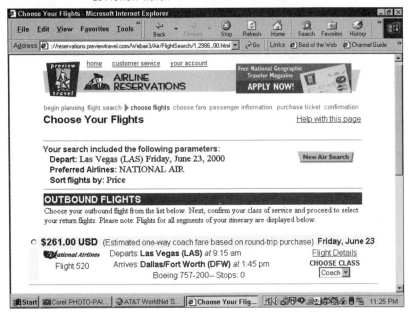

Travel sites allow you to check out and price multiple options such as departure dates, nonstops versus layovers, and vehicle sizes before making your final purchase decisions. Once you have settled on an itinerary that meets your needs, you need only use a major credit card to buy the tickets and complete the transaction. Tickets can then be sent to you via regular mail or can be issued online as e-tickets. Regardless, the Web site will provide you with a confirmation number, which you should jot down or print out for later reference. You may need this number to change or cancel your reservations at a later date.

Not all conglomerate sites provide complete travel listings for all available vendors. For example, only a few sites, such as Yahoo! Travel (travel.yahoo.com) include Southwest Airlines in their air reservations system. Check the Available Airlines area of your selected site to ensure that you are being presented with all possible options.

Many airlines update their reservation systems just after midnight in the time zones where they are based. At that time, previously reserved low fares that remain unpurchased are released. This may be an ideal time for you to go online and find the best possible airfare.

CHAPTER 10
ENTERTAINING DIVERSIONS

IN THIS CHAPTER

- Finding out "what's on" in your community, on television, and at the movies
- Enjoying Web concerts, lectures, and tours
- Getting competitive with online game playing

The Web is not only great at providing resources that make work and daily chores easier and more manageable, it's also outstanding at enlivening free time with playful and stimulating entertainment offerings. While online, you can check the TV and movie listings for your hometown, find out what cultural events are taking place nearby — and buy tickets for them online. You can even locate and reserve your attendance at events being held in other towns months in the future, scheduling your festivities for a future business trip or vacation excursion.

Even more exciting, you can participate in all sorts of Web-based entertaining diversions without ever leaving the cozy chair in front your computer. With the help of easy-to-install plug-ins, you can tune in to talk radio, watch a live theatrical performance, take a virtual walking tour of ancient ruins, or play blackjack in an online game room.

Finding Entertainment Events Near Home ... and Away!

Whether you're looking to engage your spirit and senses in some aesthetically pleasing Impressionist paintings or in a riotous rock-n-roll headbanger bash, you can use the Web to locate upcoming events of all types for virtually any city across the United States. Also, depending on the site, you can usually reserve and purchase tickets for the events you choose by completing a simple online information form and providing your credit card number to the entertainment site. Take a look at the following sites whenever you're in the mood to treat yourself to a night on the town!

- **CultureFinder:** Lycos maintains this site (`www.culturefinder.lycos.com`), which boasts access to 350,000 arts events in 1,500 cities nationwide. You select a range of dates and a city, and CultureFinder tracks down all events meeting your chosen criteria. The database includes listings and descriptions of art exhibits, theater performances, symphonies, musicals, and dance exhibitions. Showtimes and event locations are provided, along with information regarding ticket availability — sold-out shows are labeled as such. Click the <u>Order Tickets Online</u> hyperlink to buy tickets (and be prepared to pay a small service fee).

- **TicketMaster:** This commercial ticket sales organization (`www.ticketmaster.com`) you once reached by walk-in or phone has gone online with its incredible array of concert, sports, arts, and family offerings. TicketMaster, shown in Figure 10-1, is also less culturally aristocratic than CultureFinder in that it's happy to provide you access to rodeos, circuses, and wrestling matches — you know, the stuff with *real* entertainment value. The site also lists event times and locations and provides easy online ticket ordering. (Again, you pay a "per ticket convenience charge" when buying tickets from this site.)

Chapter 10: Entertaining Diversions

Figure 10-1: TicketMaster (www.ticketmaster.com) boasts extensive entertainment event listings and online ticket ordering.

- **Yahoo! Get Local:** This portion of Yahoo! gives you access to entertainment centers and events by zip code. To access Get Local, just scroll down to the bottom of the Yahoo! home page (www.yahoo.com), type the zip code of the city you want to access, and click the Enter Zip Code button. Then select the Entertainment & Arts hyperlink in the Local Web Directory area to find a list of links to entertainments offers you can further explore.

Obtaining Listings

Listings are simply schedules of what's on. If you plan on doing anything entertainment related, it's a good idea to know the details of when the action is taking place — otherwise, you might miss it! Here's how you can find all the TV and movie listings you want via the Web (and don't forget to check the Resource Center for other recommended listing sites).

Television

Statistics show that more than 99 percent of Americans own at least one television set and that they watch it an average of seven hours a day. Whether all those people actually know what they're viewing is another story! Still, *you* can stay informed of all your program options simply by going online and finding TV listings at any number of entertainment sites. One you may want to try is TV Guide (www.tvguide.com) — the granddaddy of all things television — shown in Figure 10-2. Just click the TV Listings link at the home page and provide your zip, time zone, or satellite TV provider in the designated area to retrieve your local listings.

Figure 10-2: TV Guide (www.tvguide.com) gives broadcast, cable, and satellite television listings for your area, for any program genre you choose from the featured drop-down list.

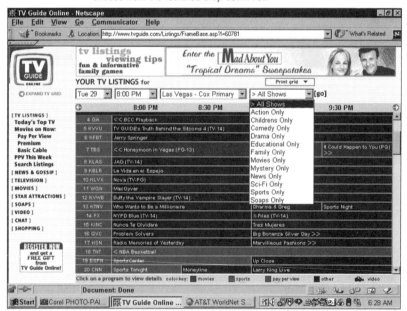

Movies

Finding movie showtimes, theaters, reviews, and trailers (previews) on the Web is a snap with sites like Moviefone (www.moviefone.com). Here, you can search for movies currently playing in your area by typing in your zip code. You can even select a genre (such as Comedy or Horror) if you've got a specific style craving. You can also read reviews of current box-office features written by big-time critics and other Web surfers like you. Best of all, taking a few minutes to download and install Quicktime or RealPlayer (see the "Participating in Net Events" section in this chapter) enables you to watch streaming video of the trailers you usually miss standing in line for popcorn!

Participating in Net Events

Squeezing playtime into your hectic life can be difficult. But the Web gives you a great way to enjoy the sights and sounds of live concerts and discussions just by logging into Internet-delivered events, or *Net events*.

One of the most common forms of Net events is the scheduled chat. The scheduled chat may feature an expert guest, such as a politician or an actor, or it may be structured as a moderated discussion on a specific topic like desert gardening or investing.

Another form of Net event you can participate in is an online broadcast of a televised gig: instead of tuning in your TV, you view the live or archived program in a little window on your computer screen, as shown in Figure 10-3.

Figure 10-3: CNN (www.cnn.com) features online broadcasts of top stories in news, entertainment, weather, and sports.

Finally, a third form of Net event that many Web users look for is online radio broadcast of music and talk channels. Tuning in online radio lets you use your computer to listen not only to channels in your local AM/FM broadcast frequencies, but also to thousands of channels beaming across the country and around the world.

To find out what Net events are taking place in the near future, try the following:

- **Access Yack** at www.yack.com. The Yack site boasts it's "Your Guide to Live Net Events," offering you a comprehensive directory of events in categories such as Yack-Sports, YackNews, and YackMusic. Most impressive about this site is its Choose an Event Channel drop-down box where you can select a link to more than 100 Web sites offering Net Events featuring specialized content. These linked sites include BigStar.com, ComedyNet, drkoop, Soap City, and more!

- **Access LiveOnTheNet** at www.liveonthenet.com. This site provides you a daily live program guide plus access to archives of events that have already taken place. Categories include Learning, Radio/TV, Religion, Sports/Rec, Webcams (including a ZooCam!), and others.

Many Net events — specifically those which play music or video — require you to download special software such as RealPlayer to participate in the event. See Chapter 4 for assistance in downloading and installing files.

Chapter 10: Entertaining Diversions 103

Online broadcasts of audio and video are typically presented in the *streaming* format. The slower your modem speed (the rate at which information flows from the Web to your computer), the choppier the transmission of sounds and images.

Taking Virtual Tours

Going for an afternoon stroll through the Louvre is a great way to toodle away the hours if you happen to be on a vacation in France. But now it's also possible for people halfway around the globe to enjoy the Louvre's priceless artwork through the magic of the Web. By taking a *virtual tour,* you can "walk" through the museum, "look" around in all directions, and "peer closely" at things you see using special zoom controls.

As the Web tourist, you control how you interact with your surroundings simply by using your mouse and the arrow keys on your keyboard. You need to download and install special software, such as QuickTime VR or Live Picture Viewer, to help your computer display the 3-D world, but not to worry . . . the tour site gives you easy directions for doing so. (See Chapter 4 for help with downloading and installing files.)

You can find virtual tours by using any major search engineand typing the keywords for whatever type of tour you want to take — for example, "**virtual tour**" **AND moon**. For a fabulous virtual moon tour be sure to check out the Lost Worlds site (www.lost-worlds.com), shown in Figure 10-4, where you can virtually stand on the lunar surface with Neil Armstrong during the Apollo 11 mission!

Figure 10-4: Lost Worlds (www.lost-worlds.com) lets you walk around on the moon, tour ancient relics, and explore other worldly (and otherworldly) wonders.

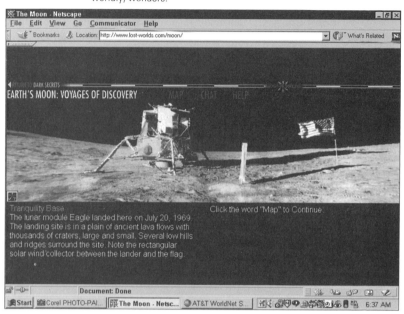

Playing Online Games

Calling all game players! If Chapter 4 got you got excited about all the incredible (and free!) games you can download from the Web, just wait until you hear this. Many Web sites, including large directories like Yahoo!, offer you a special area for online gaming where you can gather and battle it out on the Web with other players just like you. You can play everything from chess to poker to Reversi (see Figure 10-5), and you can do so at any level of game play, from novice to expert. If you're trying to learn a new game or if you're working on honing your strategies, you can also just sit and watch a game in action. And considering that typically thousands of individuals are playing online at any one time, you'll never want for an opponent to challenge your skills — or someone to just socialize with you over a gameboard! (See the Resource Center for additional game sites.)

Chapter 10: Entertaining Diversions **105**

Figure 10-5: Yahoo! Games (`games.yahoo.com`) like Reversi let you play with other Web users at any level of expertise.

CLIFFSNOTES REVIEW

Use this CliffNotes Review to practice the material covered in this book and check your understanding of strategies for finding what you want on the Web. Work through the Multiple Choice questions and the Practical Practice Projects, glancing back at the book whenever you need a helping hand. When you're finished, you can pat yourself on the back and consider yourself part of the growing breed of bona fide *Web-heads!*

Multiple Choice Questions

1. To easily return to a site you have found, you should

  a. Bookmark the site's address in your browser.

  b. Copy the site's address into a special text file you maintain on your desktop.

  c. Retrace the pathway you used to find the site so that you can remember your steps the next time.

2. To peruse a collection of increasing specific categories — and ultimately Web sites — on a general subject, you should

  a. Type the name of the subject into the Address or Location area of your Web browser and press Enter or Return.

  b. Search using a search engine.

  c. Drill down through a Web directory.

3. Using a search engine to find information is *not* a good strategy when:

  a. The information you want is very new.

  b. The information you want is broad is scope, such as **Automobiles.**

  c. The information you want may be considered obscure or very narrow in breadth.

4. To try out a sample version or limited-time trial of a software program before committing to buy the full-function product, you can download

   a. A screen saver.
   b. Shareware or freeware.
   c. A demo of the program.

5. A simple way to constantly view text of the latest news, weather, and sports headlines — while occupying the least amount of space on your desktop — is to:

   a. Open a RealPlayer window and maintain a connection to CNN Headline News.
   b. Create a personal page and keep its window minimized in the Task Bar.
   c. Download, install, and run Yahoo! News Ticker, or a similar ticker service.

6. You can use the Web to conduct a real-time conversation — in text or voice — with another person using:

   a. E-mail.
   b. An Instant Message program.
   c. A message board or bulletin board service.

7. A good starting place to find a collection of online libraries, dictionaries, encyclopedias, and maps is by:

   a. Searching for the keyword phrase **library OR dictionary OR encyclopedia OR map** in any search engine.
   b. Clicking the link for the top-level category **Reference** in any Web directory.
   c. Typing www.britannica.com in the Address or Location area of your Web browser and pressing Enter or Return.

8. Many U.S. Government Web sites can be accessed by typing which of the following into the Address or Location area of your browser and then pressing Enter or Return:

   a. www.*agency or department abbreviation*.com

   b. www.*agency or department abbreviation*.gov

   c. www.*agency or department abbreviation*.net

9. Online classifieds differ from online auctions in that:

   a. Only in auctions must you publicly bid to obtain the items up for sale.

   b. Only classifieds rate the credibility of the sellers.

   c. Only in auctions can you see pictures of available items.

10. Without leaving your computer, you can interactively view the scenery of another country or visit a museum thousands of miles away by:

    a. Joining a travel chat room.

    b. Accessing Yahoo! Travel or other travel reservations site.

    c. Taking a virtual tour.

Answers: (1) a. (2) c. (3) b. (4) c. (5) c. (6) b. (7) b. (8) b. (9) a. (10) c.

Practical Practice Projects

1. Using any of the major directories, obtain a User ID and set up a personalized page featuring headlines from your favorite news and sports sources.

2. Using any free e-mail provider (such as HotBot), set up an e-mail account. Send a practice e-mail message to a friend or relative who has an e-mail address.

3. Choose any top-level directory heading that interests you and drill down to explore the categories and Web sites it houses.

4. Find, download, and install a free screen saver that reflects your style and interests.

5. Flip through the pages of a novel you are currently reading or have completed recently. Find a word whose meaning you didn't know and look it up in an online dictionary.

6. Use a search engine to track down the lyrics (and possibly the sheet music!) for your favorite song.

7. Using any travel site, investigate the lowest airfare available for you to take a quick jaunt to any vacation destination of your choice.

8. Locate, download, and print this year's federal tax forms.

9. Look up today's stock prices for stocks you own or for a major company whose merchandise you purchase (such as Coca-Cola or Reebok).

10. Access Yahoo! Games and observe or play your favorite board or card game with fellow Web-heads.

CLIFFSNOTES RESOURCE CENTER

The learning doesn't need to stop here. Even experts at *Finding What You Want on the Web* need a little guidance in locating great sites. CliffsNotes Resource Center shows you the best of the best — links to the best information in print and online about the author and/or related works. So feel free to check this little Resource Center for tried-and-true sites, which help you find the information you want. From search engines to file respositories, this center offers suggested sites to help get you on your way.

And don't think that this is all we've prepared for you; we've put all kinds of pertinent information at www.cliffsnotes.com. Look for all the terrific resources at your favorite bookstore or local library and on the Internet. When you're online, make your first stop www.cliffsnotes.com where you'll find more incredibly useful information about *CliffsNotes Finding What You Want on the Web*.

Books

This CliffsNotes book provides information on **Finding What You Want on the Web** published by IDG Books Worldwide, Inc. If you are looking for information about the author and/or related works, check out these other publications:

CliffsNotes Exploring the Internet with Yahoo!, by Camille McCue, covers how you can use Yahoo! to access a treasure trove of online resources. IDG Books Worldwide, Inc., 1999.

CliffsNotes Getting on the Internet, by David Crowder and Rhonda Crowder, offers you quick and concise Internet guidance. IDG Books Worldwide, Inc., 1999.

Internet Directory For Dummies, 3rd Edition, by Brad Hill, provides you a catalog-style list of Web sites and summaries on subjects such as uncovering Internet and computer help online. IDG Books Worldwide, Inc., 1999.

Internet Auctions For Dummies, by Greg Holden, gets you into bidding and selling at online auction sites. IDG Books Worldwide, Inc., 1999.

Researching Online For Dummies, by Reva Basch, addresses everything from the basics of online research to topics like choosing the right search engine. IDG Books Worldwide, Inc., 1998.

It's easy to find books published by IDG Books Worldwide, Inc. You'll find them in your favorite bookstores (on the Internet and at a store near you). We also have three Web sites that you can use to read about all the books we publish:

- www.cliffsnotes.com
- www.dummies.com
- www.idgbooks.com

Internet

Check out these Web resources for more information about finding what you want on the Web:

Web Directories

About.com, www.about.com — 650 expert, human guides construct/monitor subcategories.

AltaVista, www.altavista.com — Comprehensive, professional directory and search engine.

Excite, `www.excite.com` — Enormous repository of listings categorized into channels.

LookSmart, `www.looksmart.com` — Displays entire search path on one page.

Lycos, `www.lycos.com` — Longstanding favorite housing comprehensive listings.

Infoseek, `infoseek.go.com` — An oldie, but a goodie, with a human-compiled directory.

Magellan, `magellan.excite.com` – Limited, but provides reviews for all listed sites.

Starting Point, `www.stpt.com` — Simple, three-level deep directory. Good for beginners.

Snap, `www.snap.com` — Human-compiled directory of Web sites.

Yahoo!, `www.yahoo.com` — The king of all Web site directories. All thumbs up!

Search Engines

AltaVista, `www.altavista.com` — Contains one of the largest indexes. A favorite among researchers.

Ask Jeeves, `www.askjeeves.com` — Human-powered service. Uses natural language.

Direct Hit, `www.directhit.com` — A "popularity engine." Frequently-clicked sites rank highest.

Excite, `www.excite.com` — Contains midsized index and non-Web content such as sports scores.

Google, `google.com` — Uses sophisticated next-generation technology to return the most relevant search results.

GoTo, `www.goto.com` — Companies can pay to have themselves listed higher in the results.

HotBot, `www.hotbot.com` — Most frequent "gold medalist" for successful matches.

Internet Sleuth, `www.isleuth.com` — Metacrawler that presents multiple engines and directories in one place.

Infoseek, `infoseek.go.com` — Posesses a unique search method and a human-compiled directory.

Lycos, `www.lycos.com` — Gives results from both its directory and Web crawling.

Northern Light, `www.northernlight.com` — Offers for-pay "special collection" documents inaccesble by other engines.

Yahoo!, `www.yahoo.com` — The Web's most popular service. Features directory and crawling.

Next time you're on the Internet, don't forget to drop by `www.cliffsnotes.com`. We created an online Resource Center that you can use today, tomorrow, and beyond.

Send Us Your Favorite Tips

In your quest for learning, have you ever experienced that sublime moment when you figure out a trick that saves time or trouble? Perhaps you realized you were taking ten steps to accomplish something that could have taken two. Or you found a little-known workaround that gets great results. If you've discovered a useful tip that helped you find what you wanted on the Web more effectively and you'd like to share it, the CliffsNotes staff would love to hear from you. Go to our Web site at www.cliffsnotes.com and click the Talk to Us button. If we select your tip, we may publish it as part of CliffsNotes Daily, our exciting, free e-mail newsletter. To find out more or to subscribe to a newsletter, go to www.cliffsnotes.com on the Web.

INDEX

A

A+ Art, 73
AccuWeather, 51
Acrobat file type, 36
Address Book, 61
addresses
    defined, 10
    e-mail, 56
    Web. *See* URLs; Web sites, addresses listed
advertising, 8, 9
alerts, news, 47, 48
AltaVista, 29, 78
America Online, 11, 23, 64, 65
applications, viewing downloaded documents, 40
Ask Jeeves, 29
auctions, 92, 94

B

Back button, 12, 19, 70
Beta-version software, 41
bookmarks, 13, 14
books
    online, 6
    suggested, 111, 112
Boolean operators, 33
Brittanica, 72
browsers, 10–13
browsing, 17
business
    domain names, 27
    sites, 7, 78, 79
    Web information, 77
buttons
    browser, 12, 70
    directory, 19
    Search, 13

C

Cambridge International Dictionaries, 71
chat rooms, 67, 68, 101
classes, 8
classified ads, 47, 91, 92
CliffsNotes Review, 107–110
clips, 73, 74
clubs, 62
compressed files, 36
CompuServe 2000, 11, 23
CultureFinder, 98

D

demonstration software, 41, 42, 43
dictionaries, 71
directories
    business sites, 78
    described, 15, 16, 19–22
    files, seeking, 37
    games, 104
    hierarchies, 18
    limitations, 17, 23
    listings, 112, 113
    proprietary, 23
    reference hyperlink, 70
    search engines, 24, 25
    shopping, 87
DLL files, 36
document files, 36
domain name, top-level, 27
drilling down, 18, 20, 21, 22

E

e-mail, 7, 56, 57, 59, 61, 62, 92
eBay, 92, 94
education, 8, 27
Encarta, 72, 73
encyclopedias, 7, 72, 73
entertainment
    events, 98, 99
    games, 104
    listings, 99, 100, 101
    Net events, 68, 101–103
    virtual tours, 103, 104
    Web surfing, 9
eToys, 88, 90
Excel files, 36
Excite
    described, 29
    finance, 80
    news, 45, 46
    sports, 52, 53
executable files, 36
extensions, file, 35, 36

F

Fidelity, 82
files
  downloading, 38, 40
  finding, 35–38
  software, 40, 41
finance, 7, 78–82
folders, e-mail, 62
foreign countries
  domain names, 28
Foreign Language Dictionaries, 71
free sites, 8
freeware, 40, 41
Funk and Wagnalls, 73

G

games, 104
Gap, 28
Go2Net, 30
government information, 7, 22, 27, 77, 82–84

H

hierarchies, directory, 18
history, search, 31
Hollywood.com, 73
HotBot, 29, 34, 37
Hotmail, 57, 59, 61, 62
hyperlinks
  classifieds, 91
  defined, 13
  directory, 20
  reference, 70
  search engine, 32
  shopping, 87

I

ICQ ("I seek you"), 63, 65–67
Infoseek (GO), 26, 29
instant messaging, 63, 65–67
Internet Explorer, 10–13
Internet Public Library, 75, 76
Internet Service Provider (ISP)
  browsers, 11–13
  domain names, 27
  proprietary offerings, 23
investing, online, 80–82
iVillage, 67

J

JPEG files, 36

K

keywords
  classified ads, 47
  files, 37, 42, 43
  search engines, 30, 31, 33, 34

L

language, foreign, 71
Lexical Freenet Connected Thesaurus, 71
libraries
  file types, 36
  Internet Public Library, 75, 76
  media clips, 73, 74
Library of Congress, 74, 75
listings, entertainment, 99–101
Lost Worlds, 103, 104
Lycos, 29, 67, 98

M

magazines, online, 6, 49
mall, online, 87, 88
media
  clips, 73, 74
  files, 36, 39, 41
  Net events, 102, 103
Menu bar, 12
Merriam Webster Dictionary/Thesaurus, 71
messaging, instant, 63, 65–67
Messenger, Yahoo!, 47, 48, 81, 82
metacrawler, 28, 30
Microsoft Clip Gallery Live, 74
Microsoft Network (MSN), 57, 59, 61, 62, 64
MIDI files, 36
military, 27
movies
  files, 36
  listings, 99, 101
  viewing, 8, 103
museums, 31, 103, 104
music, 8, 41, 101–103

Index

N

Nav toolbar, 12
Net events, 68, 101–103
Netscape Navigator, 10, 12, 14
networks, online, 27
news
   alerts, 47, 48
   financial, 80
   magazines, 49
   newspaper, 46, 47
   personalized, 45, 46, 52, 53
   sports, 52, 53, 54
   weather, 50, 51
News Ticker, Yahoo!, 49
non-profit groups, 27, 28
Nonsensicon, The, 71

O

operators, search, 33

P

paranormal phenomena, 21
patent office, U.S., 22
people
   chat rooms, 67, 68
   clubs, 62
   data available, 6, 55, 56
   e-mail information, 57, 59, 61, 62
   instant messaging, 63, 65–67
   White pages information, 56
personalized pages
   money, 80
   news, 45, 46
   sports, 52, 53
PowerPoint files, 36
ProgramFiles.com, 42

R

radio, 41, 102
reference materials
   described, 7, 69, 70
   dictionaries and thesauri, 71
   encyclopedias, 72, 73
   Library of Congress, 74, 75
   media clips, 73, 74
   Virtual Reference collections, 75, 76
reservations
   entertainment, 98
   travel, 94–96
rollercoasters, 22

S

screen saver, 41
Scroll bar, 12
Search button, 13, 31
search engines
   choosing, 28, 30
   described, 14, 15, 24, 25
   files, seeking, 37
   keywords, 30, 31, 33, 34
   listing, 113, 114
   shopping, 87
   virtual tours, 103
shareware, 43
Shockwave files, 36
shopping
   auctions, 92, 94
   classified ads, 91, 92
   finding goods, 86–88
   prevalence, 7
   purchasing process, 88–90
   travel reservations, 94, 95, 96
software
   browsers, 10–13
   demonstration, 41–43
   directories, 37
   distribution, 7
   downloaded files, viewing, 40
   executable files, 36
   freeware, 40, 41
   search engines, 24–28, 30–34
   shareware, 43
   Web search tools, 14
sound files, 36
sports, 52, 53, 54
stocks, monitoring, 81, 82
stores, 7, 26–28, 86–88
surfing, Web, 9
Switchboard, 56, 57

T

telephone, 41
television listings, 99, 100
thesauri, 71
TicketMaster, 98
Title bar, 12
tools, 14
TopFile, 38
travel reservations, 94–96

U

United Way, 28
URLs
  bookmarks, 14
  business and financial sites, 78
  files, 38, 43
  guessing, 25, 27, 28
  sites, specific. See Web sites, addresses listed
  stores, 86

V

video, 36, 41, 54, 101–103
Virtual Reference collections, 75, 76
virtual tours, 103, 104

W

Wave files, 36
weather, 50
Web sites
  bookmarking, 13, 14
  groupings. See directories
  prevalence, 6
  searching. See search engines
Web sites, addresses listed
  auction, 92
  chat rooms, 67
  CliffsNotes Resource Center, 111
  directories, 112, 113
  entertainment, 98, 99
  foreign country domain names, 28
  government agencies, 28, 77, 82–84
  IDG Books Worldwide, Inc., 112
  Infoseek, 26
  instant messaging, 64
  Internet Service Provider (ISP) free areas, 23
  investment, 82
  metacrawlers, 30
  Net events, 102
  news media, 45
  search engines, 29, 113, 114
  software, 39–42
  sports, 52
  stores, 26–28, 87
  travel reservations, 94, 95
  virtual tours, 103, 104
  weather, 51
  white pages, 56
  Yahoo!, 17, 19, 62
white pages, 56

WriteExpress Online Rhyming Dictionary, 72

Y

Yahoo!
  browsing, 17
  business and financial sites, 78, 79
  classifieds, 91
  clubs, 62
  described, 19, 20, 21, 22
  games, 104
  Get Local, 99
  instant messaging, 64
  People Search, 57
  search engine, 29, 32
  stocks, monitoring, 81, 82
  travel reservations, 95

Z

ZDNet, 39, 40
zip files, 36

CliffsNotes

Your shortcut to success for over 40 years

Computers and Software
Confused by computers? Struggling with software? Let *CliffsNotes* get you up to speed on the fundamentals — quickly and easily. Titles include:

Balancing Your Checkbook with Quicken®
Buying Your First PC
Creating a Dynamite PowerPoint® 2000 Presentation
Making Windows® 98 Work for You
Setting up a Windows® 98 Home Network
Upgrading and Repairing Your PC
Using Your First PC
Using Your First iMac™
Writing Your First Computer Program

The Internet
Intrigued by the Internet? Puzzled about life online? Let *CliffsNotes* show you how to get started with e-mail, Web surfing, and more. Titles include:

Buying and Selling on eBay®
Creating Web Pages with HTML
Creating Your First Web Page
Exploring the Internet with Yahoo!®
Finding a Job on the Web
Getting on the Internet
Going Online with AOL®
Shopping Online Safely